A Practical Wedding Planner

ALSO BY MEG KEENE

A Practical Wedding: Creative Ideas for Planning
a Beautiful, Affordable, and Meaningful Celebration

A

PRACTICAL WEDDING PLANNER

*A Step-by-Step Guide to
Creating the Wedding You Want
with the Budget You've Got
(Without Losing Your Mind in the Process)*

MEG KEENE

Illustrations by Eunice Moyle

DA CAPO LIFELONG BOOKS
A MEMBER OF THE PERSEUS BOOKS GROUP

Copyright © 2015 by Meg Keene
Illustrations by Eunice Moyle
Invitation design on page 91 courtesy of printablepress.com

Book Design by Linda Mark
Set in 11.5-point Goudy Oldstyle Std by the Perseus Books Group

Library of Congress Cataloging-in-Publication Data
Keene, Meg.
  A practical wedding planner : a step-by-step guide to creating the wedding you want with the budget you've got (without losing your mind in the process) / Meg Keene.
    pages cm
  Includes index.
  ISBN 978-0-7382-1842-7 (paperback)—ISBN 978-0-7382-1843-4 (e-book) 1. Weddings—Planning. 2. Weddings—Economic aspects. I. Title.
  HQ745.K444 2015
  392.5—dc23

                                                                    2015024338

First Da Capo Press edition 2015
Published by Da Capo Press
A Member of the Perseus Books Group
www.dacapopress.com

Da Capo Press books are available at special discounts for bulk purchases in the U.S. by corporations, institutions, and other organizations. For more information, please contact the Special Markets Department at the Perseus Books Group, 2300 Chestnut Street, Suite 200, Philadelphia, PA, 19103, or call (800) 810-4145, ext. 5000, or e-mail special.markets@perseusbooks.com.

10 9 8 7 6

For J., who taught me a new kind of love.

And for L., who was with me every step of the way.

Contents

YOU JUST GOT ENGAGED! OR YOU'VE been engaged for a while but are finally sitting down to plan this party. Or, hell, maybe you haven't made anything exactly official yet, but you know you want to spend your lives together.

Whichever! Ice the bubbly!

If you haven't taken some time to bliss out and enjoy this massive and wonderful decision, shut this book and go do that already. When you're ready to take a deep breath and start planning, meet me back here.

Going from the joy of a new engagement to the nitty-gritty of putting the actual celebration together can be a little like switching from drinking champagne to dumping the bucket of ice you were cooling it in over your head. Not much of

the huge wedding industry is actually set up to help couples plan weddings in the real world. The myth is that everyone (except maybe you) is employing a full-service caterer, choosing the fanciest chairs, and hiring a floral designer, a DJ, and a high-end planner to do most of the work.

The reality is that most of us have *some* limitations on what kind of wedding we can, or even want to, afford. We're aiming for weddings that more or less fit our values, without driving us into financial and emotional ruin. The wedding industry, for its part, is mostly trying to sell us more things.

In between the hard sales of pretty things and the assumption that most of us have wedding planners and unlimited funds, it turns out that there is not a ton of helpful information out there about *how* to actually put your wedding together. Not the etiquette of addressing wedding invitations (though we'll get to that), but how to figure out what you should actually do first, how to decide if you should hire a traditional caterer or rent a taco truck (or if you even want to serve a meal), and how to put together an accurate timeline of the day of the wedding.

When I was getting married, my now husband and I couldn't find much logistical advice that we trusted, so we muddled through our wedding planning, making it up as we went. Although we'd both done some work on events before, we still did not have a fantastically clear idea of what we were doing. We refrigerated our DIY flowers in a normal food fridge (don't do that; they will wilt), and I bought a last-minute vintage wedding dress because I was too overwhelmed and confused by the policies of wedding salons to bring myself to shop for a traditional dress.

In the years since then, as founder and editor in chief of APracticalWedding.com, I've tried to help countless couples plan the weddings that will leave them feeling joyful, not emotionally exhausted and broke. But as the years have gone on, I've realized that I was far from alone in planning a wedding without understanding how to get from point A to point B. And though, in my opinion, your wedding matters because of how it makes you feel, it's hard to have

a blissful experience if you can't figure out how to find a venue you can afford, avoid body shaming while wedding dress shopping, or get your wedding venue set up before your guests arrive.

In short, there is more to having a joyful wedding than the emotional guidance I offered in my book *A Practical Wedding: Creative Ideas for Planning a Beautiful, Affordable, and Meaningful Celebration.* There is also the need to understand rentals without tearing your hair out. So, over many months, I set about interviewing many wedding planners and other professionals (the saner the better) to distill the information you need most when planning a real-life wedding. This book is based on my eight years of editing APracticalWedding.com, but it's also based on the no-nonsense secrets of the trade that many awesome wedding professionals were willing to share.

At some point in writing this book, I stopped counting the number of things I wished we'd known while planning our own wedding. Because our wedding was emotional and beautiful and transcendent, even if our planning wasn't. But I hope this book serves as a tool to help you plan with fewer mistakes and less fumbling desperately in the dark than I, and most of my friends, experienced. There is no way to make wedding planning a totally painless process, but my goal is to make it far less confusing. That way you can make smarter and more informed decisions and get back to what really matters—your relationship and the people you love.

This book is not designed to be read cover to cover, detail by detail. If you have a wedding with every single element included in this book, you're not having a wedding; you're having some sort of three-ring circus. This book is meant to serve as a planning guide, and a wedding encyclopedia of sorts. If you realize you need to know how to plan for a food truck wedding, flip to those pages. If you decide you need to rent a wedding tent, dog-ear that section. And if the time has come to write your vows, peruse the tips and tricks on making them meaningful, and steal from other people's work. Plus, when you're in the real trenches of planning, you can flip through the Appendix to look at spreadsheets you might want to copy or to review checklists of (actually kind of important) stuff you might be forgetting.

Mostly, I've tried not to assume what kind of wedding you're having. Maybe you're having a church ceremony with a huge reception. Maybe you're renting a vacation home for a weekend to celebrate with your thirty closest friends. Maybe you're having a picnic in the park. Whatever wedding you decide to throw, this book provides the tools to get you there with as few tears as possible.

At least the bad tears. Happy tears? Those I can get behind.

Figuring Out What You Really Want

1

1. All you need to get married is the man, the preacher, and the dress. Or the lady, the judge, and the stylish pantsuit. Or . . . well, you get the point. But all you really need is each other, and someone to make it official in your hearts.

2. "I will remember how my wedding felt, not how my wedding looked." Repeat it to yourself over and over. Tattoo it on your arm. Write it on your fridge.

3. Figure out what you care about (and really could care less about) early in this whole process. Write it down. Come back to it when wedding planning leads you down the wayward path.

4. It's *your* wedding. But the day belongs, in part, to everyone who loves you. Make decisions accordingly.

5. Forget *pretty* for a hot second, and think about making your wedding *fun*. Because after all the big emotions of the day, the point is to have a damn fun party.

W HEN YOU GET ENGAGED, IT CAN be tempting to run out and break the news to everyone, right away. If you do that, after the first flood of congratulations, you'll quickly find yourself fielding questions on everything from your wedding date to your colors. (Welcome to other people's expectations and wedding planning.) No matter when you let the Facebook masses know, try to reserve some time just to celebrate your engagement together and figure out what the hell it is that you want out of this wedding, anyway.

Although most of this book is designed to help you through the logistical details of planning, this chapter is designed to help you figure out what kind of wedding you want in the first place.

SO YOU LIKED IT (AND YOU'RE GONNA PUT A RING ON IT)

Before you decide if you care more about a kick-ass DJ or organic catering, take some time to think about your emotional goals for this wedding. If there is one thing you should tattoo on your arm and post on your fridge, it's this simple fact: "I will not remember what my wedding looked like; I will remember what it felt like."

When the seating charts are in the trash and your wedding decor is packed away, what emotions do you want to remember? Do you want to have had a raucous dance party? A peaceful and intimate ceremony? A joyous celebration of community? After a little bit of pondering, you and your partner can brainstorm what emotions you're aiming for on each side of the Venn diagram on page 5. Then, sit down and figure out your joint emotional goals.

After that discussion, use those goals to come up with a sentence or two that I like to call "The Wedding Mission Statement." I know, coming up with a wedding

mission statement sounds somewhere between silly and self-help. But wedding planning has a way of leading you far away from where you started and what you really care about. If you know that your joint goal for the wedding is "a religious celebration of our marriage in front of our whole community, followed by a wild party" (hint: that was ours), it will help keep you focused when you've had it with planning and just want to elope instead. Likewise, if you know you want a tiny, quiet ceremony, you can come back to that when you find yourself sucked into the vortex of seventy-five family members wanting to attend.

PRIORITIES, PRIORITIES, PRIORITIES

Once you've done the work of figuring out what you want your wedding to feel like, it's time to think about what you do (and really don't) care about in the nitty-gritty of wedding planning. If you look at a traditional wedding planning timeline, you may have a slight nervous breakdown before you've read half an inch of the text. Whatever financial and emotional resources you have to devote to this wedding, chances are good they are not infinite, unlike the planning list for the modern American wedding.

Instead of giving you a to-do list, I'm giving you a "pick what you really care about" list that spans from the useful to the possibly absurd. You and your partner should each grab a different colored pen and run through this list, crossing out things you could seriously care less about, circling things that matter to you (double circling and starring things that you really value is encouraged), and scribbling in items you don't see listed. Once you've narrowed down All the Wedding Things to a smaller collection of items you actually care about, you can each fill out the list on page 7 of your top three wedding planning priorities and then try to create a joint list. You can think of this exercise as a way to figure out what makes a wedding feel like a wedding to each of you.

Remember, your priorities will change over time, but as you get lost in the weeds of "This costs *what?*" and "Your mom insists we have *that?*" you can revisit your original list to make sure you're spending your time and energy on the things that actually matter.

VENN DIAGRAM OF EMOTIONAL GOALS

EMOTIONAL GOALS

PARTNER 1   PARTNER 2

Our Wedding Mission Statement

_____

_____

_____

_____

_____

_____

_____

_____

_____

_____

_____

_____

_____

ALL THE WEDDING THINGS
(MANY OF WHICH YOU DON'T NEED)

Circle what you really care about, cross out what you don't, and add anything that's missing.

Appetizers
Attendant gifts
Attendants
Bachelor/ette parties
Beer and wine
Bouquets
Boutonnières
Bridal jewelry
Bridesmaid dresses
Bridesmaid luncheon
Budget
Cake
Cake accessories
  (topper, cutter, etc.)
Calligraphy
Centerpieces
Ceremony
Ceremony programs
Chairs
Champagne
Church
Cocktails
Colors
Corsages
Dance floor
Dance lessons
Dance party
Daytime wedding
Day-of coordinator
Decor
Decorations
Dinner party
DJ
Dress
Drinks

Engagement
  announcements
Engagement party
Engagement photos
Engagement ring(s)
Extended family
Favors
Flatware
Flowers
Flower girls (and boys)
Food
Formal dress
Friends (lots of)
Getaway car
Grand exit
Groom's cake
Guest list
Guest book
Hair
Hometown
Honeymoon
Hotel
Indoors
Invitations
Late-night snacks
Lighting
Linens
Local
Makeup
Marriage license
Music
Next-day brunch
Nighttime wedding
Non-alcoholic
  beverages

Officiant
Outdoors
Passports (for an in-
  ternational wedding
  or honeymoon)
Photo booth
Photographer
Premarital counseling
Private time together
Reception band
Reception playlist
Registry
Rehearsal dinner
Religious ceremony
Rings
Ring bearer
Salon services (facials,
  tanning, waxing, etc.)
Save-the-dates
Shoes
Showers
Sit-down meal
Theme
Toasts
Transportation
Tux or suit
Ushers
Veil
Venue
Videographer
Vows
Website
Wedding planner
Welcome baskets
Vows

WEDDING PLANNING PRIORITIES

After looking over the previous (overly long) list, try to pick out which three things matter most to each of you personally, and then discuss your joint priorities for the wedding.

Top 3 Wedding Planning Priorities: Partner One

_____

_____

_____

Top 3 Wedding Planning Priorities: Partner Two

_____

_____

_____

Our Joint Top 3 Wedding Planning Priorities

_____

_____

_____

EXTRA CREDIT: BRINGING IN THE FAMILY

Once you have figured out what your joint planning priorities are, it can save you a lot of heartache to ask involved family members the same questions. If the one thing your dad really wants is chicken at dinner, and your mom desperately wants the family pastor to perform the service, it's helpful to know that from the start. Your dad might not get poultry and your mom might not get religion, but if you don't know what people care about, you'll end up in a tangled confusion of assumptions and obligations, without the tools you need to have clear conversations and make good compromises.

Since every couple has different family setups I've included lists for four family groupings, though your numbers may vary.

Top 3 Wedding Planning Priorities: Family Grouping One

_____

_____

_____

Top 3 Wedding Planning Priorities: Family Grouping Two

_____

_____

_____

Top 3 Wedding Planning Priorities: Family Grouping Three

_____

_____

_____

Top 3 Wedding Planning Priorities: Family Grouping Four

_____

_____

_____

PUTTING IT IN ORDER

Once you've cobbled together a rough idea of your goals, you need a basic plan of attack. I struggled to come up with a wedding planning checklist for this book because, well, most wedding planning checklists are insane. I have one that runs a cool six pages, with everything from booking your pre-wedding spray tan (what?) to buying stamps for your wedding invitations (something that, trust me, you'll remember to do sooner or later). So instead, this is a one-page general order of wedding planning operations (in an ideal world). We don't live in an ideal world, so you won't necessarily approach things exactly in this way, and you might not be doing everything listed here. But this is a good guideline to stick on your fridge to turn to when you wonder, "Well . . . what next?"

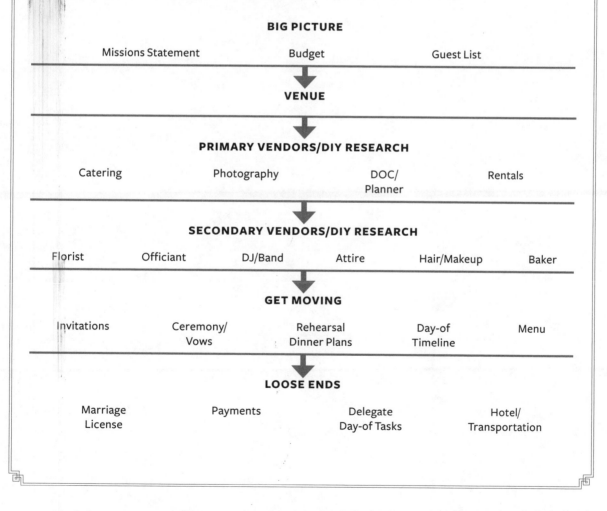

BIG PICTURE

Missions Statement	Budget	Guest List

↓

VENUE

↓

PRIMARY VENDORS/DIY RESEARCH

Catering	Photography	DOC/ Planner	Rentals

↓

SECONDARY VENDORS/DIY RESEARCH

Florist	Officiant	DJ/Band	Attire	Hair/Makeup	Baker

↓

GET MOVING

Invitations	Ceremony/ Vows	Rehearsal Dinner Plans	Day-of Timeline	Menu

↓

LOOSE ENDS

Marriage License	Payments	Delegate Day-of Tasks	Hotel/ Transportation

HOW TO HAVE A FUN WEDDING

The wedding industry is built on selling you a pretty wedding. The dress, the tux, the flowers, the invitations, the decor—all of it paints a pretty picture, but it contributes very little to the actual experience of the day. Because, as my husband wisely pointed out to me a month before our wedding, pretty isn't an emotion. And how your wedding looks and how your wedding feels are two very different (and nearly unrelated) things. I don't say this to talk you out of getting a kick-ass outfit, or investing time in finding decorations that you love. I say this to remind you to take a time-out early on to think about how to make your wedding enjoyable.

Chances are, you already know how to throw a really fun party. Those same principles apply to weddings. Here are some tips and tricks to remember.

- **Invite people you love.** The single most important element of your wedding is the people. When you walk away from a wedding, you think about the conversations you had, the people you caught up with, and the vibe of all those awesome folks in one room. No matter how big or how small your celebration, think of the people first, and make everything else secondary.
- **Fit your wedding to your crowd.** The goal is to balance your emotional needs on your wedding day with being a good host. Make sure you're planning a party that you'll be comfortable at, but that has elements that your guests enjoy as well. (That may mean mixing some Motown into your indie rock playlist.)
- **Let people know what to expect.** Guests are surprisingly good at rolling with the (non-traditional wedding) punches, as long as they know what they're getting into up front. If you're having a reception where you're only serving cake and punch, let people know on the invite. They'll come with full stomachs, ready to have a good time. (Or they'll decide they're not into it and won't come at all. Guests are grownups like that.) Use your invitation, a wedding website if you have one, and word of mouth to let people know what kind of party they're in for.
- **Make your guests feel taken care of.** There is something a little vulnerable about showing up at a wedding where you don't know many people and putting the next six hours of your life in the hosts' hands. You hope they'll feed you well and sit you next to nice people, but you never quite know. There are as many ways you can take care of your guests as there are weddings, from leaving welcome notes at the hotel to providing a way for guests to get to know each other (like name tags with a note about how you know the couple at a welcome dinner), to a seating

chart. (For more on seating charts, see pages 171–173.)

- **Feed people on time.** If I had to pick the number one rule for all weddings ever, it would be this: Feed people. At mealtimes. With enough food. Hangry guests are not happy guests.

- **And finally, have fun.** The single best thing you can do to make your wedding fun is just to relax and enjoy it. Guests are paying careful attention to the wedding couple and taking their cues from them. If you're relaxed, they'll relax. If you're dancing, they'll dance. If you're having the time of your life, they will, too.

THE PERFECT IS THE ENEMY OF THE GOOD

One final note, before you dive into the thick of planning. There is a tendency to think that because the ritual of the wedding is meaningful and personal that every single element needs to be painstakingly researched and imbued with meaning. It can be hard to pick between two photographers you like because you have the tantalizing sense that the *perfect* photographer is just around the corner. You don't want to bite the bullet to pick a wedding invitation because you're not sure if the invites reflect your personalities and union in a way that will stand the test of (all) time.

When you find yourself not making a decision because you can't be sure it's the best one, stop for a minute. Remember that the perfect is the enemy of the good, and if you spend forever trying to make the best selection, the really good choice will pass you by. (And you'll slowly descend into madness.)

Your wedding won't be perfect. It won't be an exact reflection of your personalities. It won't even be timeless. It will, simply, be the moment when you got married. And that is perfect enough.

Guests First, Budget Second

1. People first. Figure out who you love and want with you on your wedding day. Then figure out how you can afford to host them.

2. You can get married on whatever budget you've got, if you're willing to get creative.

3. Do a reality check. Throwing a party for a lot of people can add up quickly. So though you can have an awesome wedding on whatever budget number you dreamed up, it might not be the wedding you originally hoped for. Figure out what your dollars will buy you, and then adjust your budget (or your expectations) accordingly.

4. Think big picture. What do you remember about the last great wedding you went to? The people and the amazing DJ? Or the centerpieces and the cocktail napkins? I'm pretty sure we all know the answer to that question is, "I can't actually remember a single wedding centerpiece ever."

5. Guest lists are hard. It's not just you.

◆

ONCE YOU HAVE A CLEAR SENSE OF what you're shooting for with this party, then it's time to talk numbers. Specifically, two sets of numbers. First, how many people you think you'll realistically have at this wedding. And second, how much cash you think you'll have to spend. Those two numbers will drive most of your planning decisions.

DON'T START BY CUTTING YOUR GUEST LIST

Most of the wedding industry will tell you that if you have a limited wedding budget (and really, who doesn't have a wedding budget with some limits?) the first thing you should do is cut your guest list, so you can afford more things. I'm going to give you the opposite advice. I think most of us throw weddings so we can celebrate with our people (the glitter and flowers and tulle are just really nice side effects of that celebrating). Because of that, I think you should start with your loved ones and work backward.

In her book *Miss Manners' Guide to a Surprisingly Dignified Wedding*, etiquette sage Miss Manners wisely suggests that you should start by figuring out how many people you want to invite, and then figure out what you can feed them. When you and your partner sit down for a heart-to-heart, you might decide to have only your nearest and dearest around you, or that you have two huge families and a lot of friends you want to celebrate with. Whatever you decide, try not to let budget worries deter you too much. No matter what the wedding industry tells you, guests don't come to your wedding for the fancy meal or the perfect decorations; they come to the wedding for the two of you. And if what you can afford to feed them is cake and punch . . . well, who doesn't like cake and punch?

QUESTIONS TO DISCUSS WITH YOUR PARTNER

Putting together a guest list is an odd mix of logic, philosophy, and (God help us) family dynamics. Before you jump in, flailing a pen around and assuming everyone is on exactly the same page, here are some questions to talk through with your partner and your loved ones.

- What are your goals for your wedding? Tiny and intimate? Huge and intimate? A celebration of community? A celebration of culture? What does that mean for your guest list?
- Realistically, for each of you, roughly how many people do you have to invite? How many people will each of your parents want to invite?
- Will you be setting limits on how many guests your parents can invite? (Related: Are your parents paying for the wedding? How much of the wedding are they paying for?)
- Will you be including plus-ones for single guests?
- Will you be including kids?
- How many of your guests are local? How many of your guests will be traveling for the wedding?

Once you get through these questions, you should have a rough idea of the number you're looking at. This number might be exactly what you expected, or it may be a bit of a shock. If you find yourself staring at a three-hundred-person guest list, and you know that simply doesn't meet your goals for what you want your wedding to feel like (or what you can honestly afford, even if you are only feeding the hungry hordes cake), now is the time to reevaluate. If you had to make A, B, and C lists, what would that look like? If you had to tell your parents (or yourself) that there are limits on who they could invite, how would that go? Of the variety of plans and compromises available to you, which seems the most palatable?

THE GUEST LIST SPREADSHEET

As you're starting the process of creating a guest list, start a spreadsheet. (See a sample in the Appendix.) Your spreadsheet should contain all of the obvious facts, but it's also a great place to collect as much information as you can. Think of this as your one-stop shop for all information wedding guest related.

Your spreadsheet should include a variety of information, including the following.

- Name (and honorifics, if you're using them)
- Address
- E-mail and phone number if you can get them (Chances are you'll need that later when people forget to RSVP.)

- A number for each invitee (You'll include this as a tiny pencil mark on their RSVP cards, for when people forget to include their names.)
- Likelihood of attendance (Yes, you're inviting your bedridden great-aunt who lives across the country, but we both know she's not going to come.)
- Events guests are invited to (Bridal shower? Rehearsal dinner? Just the wedding?), and number of people from their parties attending each event
- Dietary restrictions and food choices
- Anything else you might need to track (Guests' hotel accommodations? Dates of arrival? What you need to know will vary depending on your wedding.)

⁎⁎ PRO TIP ⁎⁎

If you're considering using online RSVPs as one of your options, there are several good Web-based services that can tally and track all of this information for you. Some of them also allow you to manage guest communication. Because managing RSVPs and communicating with guests is inevitably a bigger job than you expect, these services often end up worth a little cash outlay.

The Imperfect Science of RSVP Response Rates

The final logical question to consider is how many of those invited guests will actually come. Don't fool yourself into thinking that because everyone loves you, your RSVP rate will be nearly 100 percent. Everyone *does* love you, but there are also things like travel costs and babysitters and unchangeable plans to consider.

So how do you guesstimate an RSVP rate? The best way to do this is simply by knowing your crowd. You know if your family always turns up for everything, or if your grad school friends are kind of flaky and broke.

That said, it never hurts to have some hard estimates in your pocket, so let's do the numbers. Here are average RSVP rates that wedding planners use for back-of-the-envelope calculations. Construct equations as you will, remembering to exclude people who were only invited as honorary guests and will not be attending.

- Average Total RSVP Rate: 75 percent attendance
- Local Guests: 85–90 percent attendance
- Non-Local Guests: 65–75 percent attendance (Note: How awesome is your location? How easy/cheap is it to get to? Is your wedding during a holiday? Depending on those factors, your rate might be decidedly higher.)
- Family: 85 percent attendance
- Friends: 50 percent attendance
- Weddings Under Fifty Guests: 90 percent attendance

WEDDING PARTY BASICS

The wedding industry has a lot to say about wedding parties—both what they are and also what they are not. Best advice? Forget the rules.

Your wedding party, in whatever form it takes, is simply the group of people that you want to honor during a big moment in your life. They are the people whom you want supporting you in this high-joy, high-stress, high-emotion moment. They may include a lifelong best friend or a family member whom you're not that close to but really want to honor. Regardless, they're your people, and you're choosing them because you love them.

Here are some general guidelines for thinking about, and picking, your wedding party.

> They can be mixed-gender groups. Men don't have to only stand up with men; women don't have to only stand up with women.
> They can be various ages. You want to have your granny as your flower girl? Your tween sister as your maid of honor? Your dad as your groomsman? Do it.

> Nobody has to wear matching clothes. Or shoes. Or earrings. Of course they can if you want, but they don't have to. (For more, see pages 117–120.)
> The same numbers of people don't need to stand up for both members of the couple. If your partner has one lifelong best friend, and you have six best girlfriends and sisters, that's perfectly okay. People are more likely to notice that there are five semi-strangers standing up with you than if you have uneven numbers.
> Any number of people is okay. Although my general guideline is that (pending a teeny-tiny semi-elopement) you generally want more guests than wedding party members, there really are no hard-and-fast rules. You do you.
> You can honor people who are not in your wedding party. They can do readings at the ceremony, or witness the marriage license, or act as ushers.
> Your wedding party may help you put this wedding together (and throw you a shower and a few extra parties). And they may not. It's okay. People's personalities don't profoundly change during wedding planning, and your flaky sister is likely going to stay as unreliable as ever. Although you may want to plan for that, it doesn't mean you shouldn't include her.
> No matter what the planning books tell you, wedding parties do not have to add to your expenses. Your best people are in this for love, not gifts or parties. If you want to give a gift, a frame (with a promise of a photo

of the two of you together on the wedding day) will more than suffice . . . as will a heartfelt note of thanks.
> Your wedding party can be unofficial. You can call them your non-bridesmaids, or your bridal brigade, or just your team. They don't have to stand up during the ceremony, or wear special outfits, or hold flowers. You can create your support system in whatever way works for you.
> Asking people to be in your wedding party is an honor. Un-asking them is hardly ever worth it, unless you're looking to end a friendship. So ask wisely.
> You don't have to have a wedding party. This commitment is about the two of you.
> And remember, you picked them because you love them. Demonstrate that with your actions.

SETTING YOUR BUDGET

Now it's time to talk budget. How fun for everyone! (I kid, I kid.) You have a general idea of how many people you might, theoretically, like to have at this party. Now, how much will you spend on celebrating with them?

Chances are good that the money you spend on your wedding will come from a variety of sources—whether that's from your savings and your partner's savings, or from parents, family members, or other loved ones. The trick is to figure out a budget balance that works for everyone involved.

Here are some common ways that couples budget for weddings.

- The couple pays on their own
- One (or multiple) sets of parents pay
- The couple and one (or multiple) sets of parents pay
- People offer to contribute flat amounts
- People offer to pay for specific budget items
- Different parties pay in equal percentages
- Different parties pay what they can

The Sky Is the Limit

In almost all cases, there is a way to meet your basic wedding goals with your budget, provided that you're willing to get creative with your expectations. If you want to get together a hundred of your favorite people and feed them a meal but you only have $2,000 to spend, it can probably be done—once you drop all the loaded expectations that come with the word "wedding" and just think "party." You may be serving them pizza or tacos, and they may be eating on their laps in your backyard, but if you're determined and flexible, you can make it work.

That said, it's important to keep in mind that weddings are real life, and in real life, things cost money. I've seen too many couples set arbitrary budgets and then try to force those budgets to meet rigid expectations. This nearly always ends in tears.

The truth is, when you start planning a wedding, chances are you just don't know what things will cost (and you're probably rather hopefully underestimating prices). This might mean that your original budget turns out to be unrealistic when you price out the wedding that you want to have. If that happens, you have two options. You can reimagine your wedding, and make it work on the money you have. Or you may find that you need to change your budget number to something that can realistically fit your original goals. Only you know what the right choice is, but remember that there is no moral superiority in sticking to your original (and possibly

---

⤙ PRO TIP ⤚

Liz Coopersmith of Silver Charm Events offers this guidance: "I have this thing called the Olive Garden Rule. Most people don't think of the Olive Garden as wedding-caliber food, but consider that there, an appetizer, a salad, and a few glasses of wine will cost about $50 per person. Transition that to a hundred guests, and it would cost $5,000 to serve Olive Garden at your wedding. Having a wedding at any budget is possible, but compare things to real life, and think about how money spends."

uninformed) budget. The point is to figure out what works best for you and your loved ones, and skip the guilt.

Taking It to the Bank

Beyond knowing who is going to pay what, it's important to know what money is coming in, and when. Are you paying for your wedding with money that is already in a savings account somewhere? Are you planning on saving while you're planning? Are you sticking to a specific final budget, or just paying what seems reasonable, when you can? Will your parents write checks up front, will they write checks as needed, or will they give you a check the night before the wedding? If you're expecting money to come in gradually, are you comfortable occasionally using credit cards to tide you over till it does?

Figuring out wedding cash flow can mean asking a lot of uncomfortable questions. After someone agrees to give you a hefty sum of money, you generally don't want to follow up by asking, "Great, WHEN?" But with wedding planning, you have to. Writing check after check is stressful enough. Trying to pay for things with money that you're not sure will ever arrive is much worse.

A Post-it Note Does Not a Budget Make

You know how I set our wedding budget? On a Post-it. I wrote the big number at the

---

---

top, and then scribbled some sums for the major items like venue, food, and photography, and I had some money left over for "other stuff."

Because you should (really) do what I say, and not what I did, may I suggest that the sample budget spreadsheet in the Appendix is a good tool to help you keep track of all the moving parts. However, here are some general budgeting principles worth following.

The 123s of Budget Setting

To help you come up with a better (and actually less stressful) budgeting plan, I've collected some best practices from wedding planners, who've seen every budget (and budget misstep) under the sun.

- **Set a target number, and then create an actual budget.** It's easy to think, "Oh, that's a lot of money; it'll probably all work out." Maybe . . . not. If you want to avoid tears at the finish line, take a good long look at what it means to sign on the line for a venue and food contract that's 70 percent of your budget, or to hire that expensive photographer you love and just have to have. Compromises are good, but they don't happen by magic.
- **Figure out your priorities and where you want to cut.** If you know that you're willing to spend a large percentage of your budget on good food, make sure you figure out the other areas where you're willing to spend less (or nothing at all).
- **Don't forget to budget for items that are important to you.** Not everything you care about will be listed in a sample wedding budget. So make sure that if you want to pay for plane tickets for a few of your friends, get a second reception dress, or have a super-cool photo booth, you add those costs to your budget up front.
- **Allow wiggle room.** Once you figure out your target budget, build in a 5 to 10 percent slush fund. Because, yes, something will go wrong at the last minute, or you'll underestimate some cost, or you'll just get tired and want to throw money at a problem to make it go away.

The Devil Is Not in the Details

It's easy to get caught up in the minutia. Should we go with the letterpressed invitations or the digitally printed ones? Should we pay extra for these beautiful fresh-flower centerpieces? Do we need a gluten-free cake to go with our regular wedding cake?

But the truth is, details are not how we experience weddings. When you think back on weddings you loved, chances are you can't remember a single centerpiece. You may not even remember what the wedding dress looked like other than a vague, "It was . . . white . . . and . . . short? I think?" What you do remember are the big things—that the ceremony was moving, how fun the crowd was, that they had a bonfire, that you got to eat really yummy cake.

So when your wedding budget is stressing you out, and you feel like you can't possibly afford all of the details, remember what Meg Hotchkiss of La Vie En Rose Events says: "That wedding would have been so much better if they had personalized cocktail napkins. That sentence has never been said until right now." And it will never be said again.

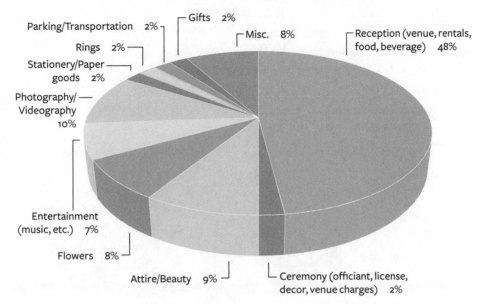

THE "AVERAGE" WEDDING BUDGET PIE CHART

Parking/Transportation 2%
Gifts 2%
Misc. 8%
Reception (venue, rentals, food, beverage) 48%
Rings 2%
Stationery/Paper goods 2%
Photography/ Videography 10%
Entertainment (music, etc.) 7%
Flowers 8%
Attire/Beauty 9%
Ceremony (officiant, license, decor, venue charges) 2%

THE MYTH OF THE WEDDING BUDGET PIE CHART

When you start researching wedding budgets, you'll see a nearly identical "average" wedding budget pie chart over and over. It looks something like the chart above.

There is helpful information in that chart—for example, if you're using a traditional venue and caterer, it probably will take up about 50 percent of your budget. But the problem is, these numbers are hard to apply in the real world, because real weddings don't tend to work out quite this neatly.

If you have enough money to spend on your wedding that you don't need to make any hard decisions—if you can afford the photographer you love, the live band you want, *and* that fancy wedding dress—then

it's true that those things might take up 9 percent and 7 percent of your budget, respectively. But for most of us, wedding planning is a series of Hobson's choices. You can have the nice photographer, or you can have the good DJ, or you can have half-DIY versions of both. That means that real-life wedding budgets usually look less like averages and more like reflections of what we personally care about. As, of course, they should.

So instead of one marginally useful pie chart, here are a few pages of pie charts. These are real wedding budgets from APW readers, in a range of price points, styles, and locations. There is no one way to build your wedding budget, so let these inspire you to figure out what you and your partner want.

REAL WEDDING BUDGET PIE CHARTS

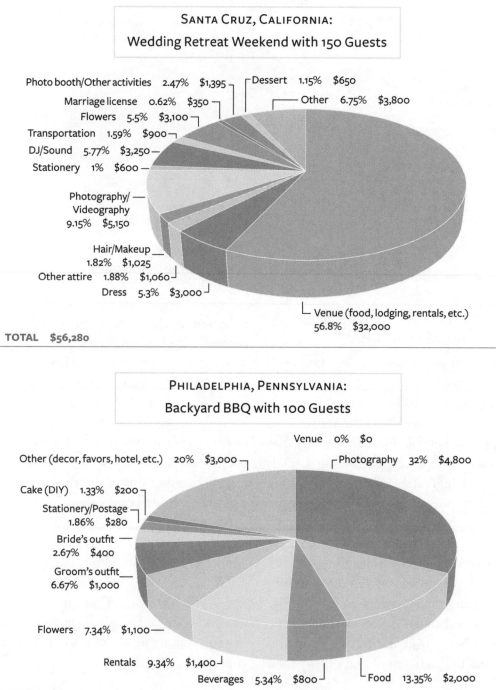

Santa Cruz, California:
Wedding Retreat Weekend with 150 Guests

Photo booth/Other activities   2.47% $1,395
Marriage license   0.62% $350
Flowers   5.5% $3,100
Transportation   1.59% $900
DJ/Sound   5.77% $3,250
Stationery   1% $600
Photography/ Videography   9.15% $5,150
Hair/Makeup   1.82% $1,025
Other attire   1.88% $1,060
Dress   5.3% $3,000

Dessert   1.15% $650
Other   6.75% $3,800
Venue (food, lodging, rentals, etc.)   56.8% $32,000

TOTAL $56,280

Philadelphia, Pennsylvania:
Backyard BBQ with 100 Guests

Venue   0% $0
Other (decor, favors, hotel, etc.)   20% $3,000
Photography   32% $4,800
Cake (DIY)   1.33% $200
Stationery/Postage   1.86% $280
Bride's outfit   2.67% $400
Groom's outfit   6.67% $1,000
Flowers   7.34% $1,100
Rentals   9.34% $1,400
Beverages   5.34% $800
Food   13.35% $2,000

TOTAL $14,980

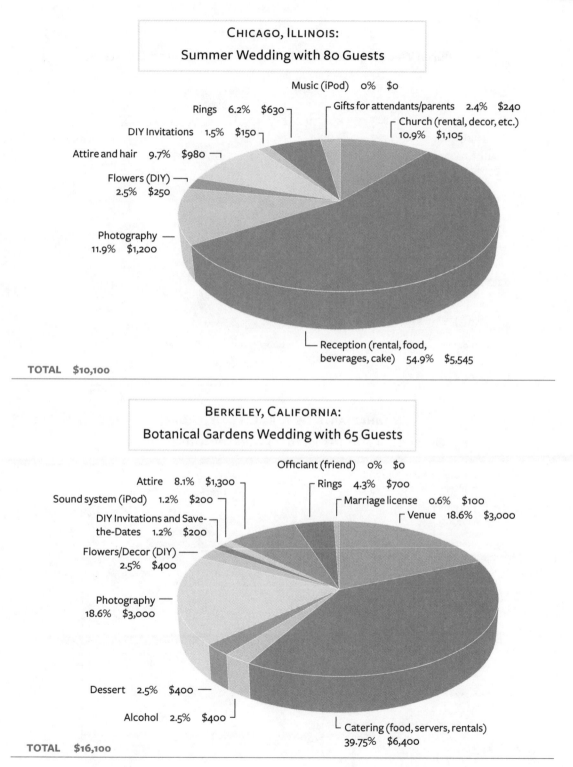

CHICAGO, ILLINOIS:
Summer Wedding with 80 Guests

Music (iPod)   0% $0

Rings   6.2% $630

Gifts for attendants/parents   2.4% $240

DIY Invitations   1.5% $150

Church (rental, decor, etc.)
10.9% $1,105

Attire and hair   9.7% $980

Flowers (DIY)
2.5% $250

Photography
11.9% $1,200

Reception (rental, food,
beverages, cake)   54.9% $5,545

TOTAL $10,100

BERKELEY, CALIFORNIA:
Botanical Gardens Wedding with 65 Guests

Officiant (friend)   0% $0

Attire   8.1% $1,300

Rings   4.3% $700

Sound system (iPod)   1.2% $200

Marriage license   0.6% $100

DIY Invitations and Save-
the-Dates   1.2% $200

Venue   18.6% $3,000

Flowers/Decor (DIY)
2.5% $400

Photography
18.6% $3,000

Dessert   2.5% $400

Alcohol   2.5% $400

Catering (food, servers, rentals)
39.75% $6,400

TOTAL $16,100

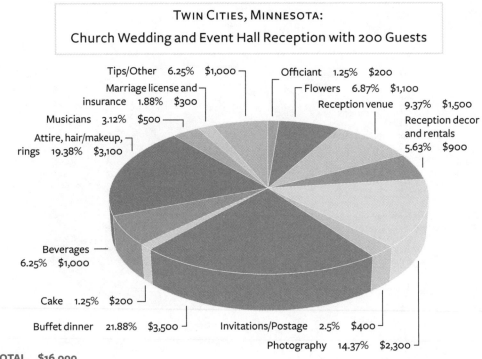

TWIN CITIES, MINNESOTA:
Church Wedding and Event Hall Reception with 200 Guests

Tips/Other 6.25% $1,000
Marriage license and insurance 1.88% $300
Musicians 3.12% $500
Attire, hair/makeup, rings 19.38% $3,100
Beverages 6.25% $1,000
Cake 1.25% $200
Buffet dinner 21.88% $3,500
Invitations/Postage 2.5% $400
Photography 14.37% $2,300
Officiant 1.25% $200
Flowers 6.87% $1,100
Reception venue 9.37% $1,500
Reception decor and rentals 5.63% $900

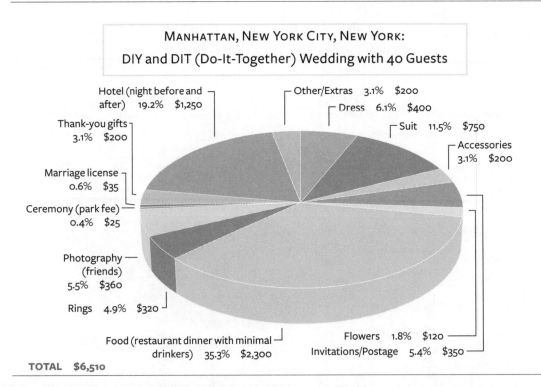

MANHATTAN, NEW YORK CITY, NEW YORK:
DIY and DIT (Do-It-Together) Wedding with 40 Guests

Hotel (night before and after) 19.2% $1,250
Thank-you gifts 3.1% $200
Marriage license 0.6% $35
Ceremony (park fee) 0.4% $25
Photography (friends) 5.5% $360
Rings 4.9% $320
Food (restaurant dinner with minimal drinkers) 35.3% $2,300
Flowers 1.8% $120
Invitations/Postage 5.4% $350
Other/Extras 3.1% $200
Dress 6.1% $400
Suit 11.5% $750
Accessories 3.1% $200

TOTAL $6,510

From the Ballroom to the Beach:
Location and Logistics

3

1. You can get married basically anywhere. A cliff overlooking the ocean, a ballroom, a barn, a park. Start reimagining the places you can have a wedding and see where that takes you.

2. When you throw a wedding in a non-traditional space, you will have a lot of logistics to manage. You might well have to deal with (and pay for) everything from insurance, to tables and chairs, to bathrooms, to disposing of the trash. Figure out what you can manage. If you decide to get married in an all-inclusive wedding hall? Consider that a good call, too.

3. Many venues have limits on the kinds of food and alcohol you can serve. Make sure you understand the limits before you sign a contract.

4. Make sure you know what rentals you might need, and what they might cost you. That big open field might be cheap, but if you need to rent a tent—and chairs, and tables, and…—it's going to get pricey, fast.

5. Finding a wedding venue can be stressful. And expensive. That is normal.

◆

DECIDING ON YOUR WEDDING VENUE is big.

Before you've signed on the dotted (venue contract) line, the sky is the limit. Up to that moment, you're still having all the weddings—the courthouse elopement, the hippie wedding barefoot in the middle of a field, the evening candlelight dinner in a ballroom. But when you commit to a venue, you're committing to *your* wedding. Suddenly, you'll know more or less what party you're having, though the balloon colors and food may vary.

Plus, it's an expensive decision. Those average wedding budget pie charts will almost always tell you that your venue and food combined make up, on average, 50 percent of your budget. And though those budget overviews can often feel a little bit useless, they tend to be more or less right on this. Together, those two decisions will usually make up about half of your wedding, either budget- or logistics-wise.

All that can make searching for a wedding venue stressful. But until you pick your venue (and in so doing, pick your date), you can't move on to more fun stuff, like the tulle and flowers. So let's walk through finding the right spot for your particular celebration.

FIGURE OUT WHAT YOU WANT IN A VENUE

When you start planning, it can seem like the world (or at least Pinterest) is your oyster. But you're only planning one wedding, and once you understand your logistical reality, your options will not be as wide open as you might have thought (and thank God for that). Before you start looking for a venue, there are some basic things you want to decide on. (If you're not sure on some of these points, early venue research may answer some of these questions for you.)

- Where are you getting hitched? Where you live? One of your hometowns? A remote destination?
- How many people are you inviting, and how many people do you expect to actually come? (More on response numbers on page 18.)
- What is your overall budget goal, and roughly how much of that can you allocate for your venue?
- What are your mandatory requirements, and what is your dream list for your venue? (Outside space? Good light? Place for a ceremony and reception? Space for 300?)
- What are your requirements for food service? Do you want to bring in your own food? Have a picnic? Not be limited to a single caterer?

TRADITIONAL VERSUS NON-TRADITIONAL VENUES

There are two basic types of wedding venues: traditional and non-traditional. Each has advantages and disadvantages.

TRADITIONAL VENUES

- Are experienced at doing weddings, and hence are far less labor intensive

- Can cost more up front
- Generally have more things included in the price (such as commercial kitchens, bathrooms, trash cans, brooms, venue staff, and sometimes even tables and chairs)
- Usually have a dance floor
- Have all legal requirements, from permits to sound ordinances, already met
- Often will have a very specific list of rules (worked out from years of doing events like weddings)
- May feel less personal or creative

NON-TRADITIONAL VENUES

- Often will have a much lower cost (at least up front)
- Can feel original and unique
- Are not set up for weddings, so may require you to build your event from scratch
- Usually require you to do much more planning
- May have many additional costs (from rentals to staff to insurance)

HOW TO FIND A TRADITIONAL VENUE

If you know you're looking for a more traditional wedding venue, your search process should be relatively straightforward. There are many Internet guides and directories of wedding venues. You'll want to search out venues that fit your basic requirements.

To simplify this process, wedding planner Katie Wannen of The Plannery suggests that you may want to keep a spreadsheet of the following information. (See a sample of this spreadsheet in the Appendix.)

The basics:

- Name of venue
- Location
- Dates available
- Rates
- Website

The details:

- Capacity—Note that if you are doing a cocktail party instead of a sit-down meal, you'll likely be able to fit more people in the space.
- Restrictions—There can be restrictions on everything from sound, to hours, to parking, to . . . you name it.
- Parking and transportation—Is it free? Is it on public transit? Does a venue require hiring a valet or other parking service?
- Facility extras—Is there anything included in the rental? Tables, chairs, A/V equipment, etc.
- Extra fees, extra hours—Are there hidden fees? Will you need to add extra hours onto your bill?
- Caterer—Is there a preferred list? An in-house caterer? Can you use any traditional caterer? Can you use non-traditional caterers like food trucks?

- Alcohol limitations—Can you bring in your own booze? Does the venue require that you use a particular bar company?
- Kitchen space—What is provided?
- My cost—This final line will involve some research, but once you come up with what additional rentals you'll need, what additional fees you'll need to pay, what staff you might have to hire, and maybe even a rough estimate of catering costs, total it all up to better compare venues.

VENUES AND CATERING COSTS

Many venues have specific rules around the food and alcohol that you can serve at events, and those rules will significantly affect the overall cost. Venues that only allow particular caterers can get pricey quickly (though all-inclusive venues can sometimes be an exception to this rule, see pages 30–31). Similarly, venues that let you bring in your own booze can often save you a lot of money. And keep in mind that any venue that minimizes your need for rentals (if they include anything from tables and chairs to bathrooms and commercial kitchens) will save you on both additional cost and trouble.

WHITTLING DOWN YOUR OPTIONS

Once you've done the initial research, your options may feel far less overwhelming than you might expect. Take your narrowed-down list and arrange some venue visits. Bring the list of venue walk-through questions (pages 42–43), and remember to listen to your gut. Sometimes, after all that research, finding a venue is as easy as walking into the space and getting the feeling, "This one's for me."

Finally, when signing a venue contract, read every line (more about contracts on page 49–50). Make sure you know exactly what the cancellation terms are, and what insurance the venue does (and does not) cover for you. Use your common sense, and your negotiating skills, and remember that if it looks like a bad contract, it's probably a bad contract.

ALL-INCLUSIVE VENUES

Between the wedding industry's emphasis on personal weddings and the indie wedding industry's focus on unique weddings, it can be hard to take the idea of the all-inclusive venue seriously. "A wedding factory? Where there are six weddings a day and they're all done the same way? Why would I ever consider it?"

Well. For some very good reasons, actually.

All-inclusive venues span from banquet hall complexes to resorts. Unlike more traditional wedding venues, here you generally pick a package you'd like, talk to the preselected vendors about your preferred cake flavors, menu, and flowers . . . and then show up in some hot outfits and get hitched. Because all-inclusive venues work with vendors on a large number of weddings, they are generally able to get good deals, and they pass on those deals to the consumer. So even though you won't have a ton of options, you will often get a good price, with minimal stress. As Julia Henning, vice president of sales and marketing at Wedgewood Wedding and Banquet Centers, puts it, "We're good for the client who wants something nice but doesn't want to spend too much. If you're saving for a house, or for life, you can get something nice without having a Kim Kardashian budget."

All-inclusive venues can be great if you're busy and you don't care about endless personalization, but instead just want someone to solve the problems for you. If you're looking at an all-inclusive venue, you should ask the questions in the venue walk-through list on pages 42–43. However, in addition to those questions, here are some specific concerns to consider:

- What additional fees will be added to your bill?
- How much can you tailor packages? Can you cut elements that you don't want to pay for?
- What vendors are included? What vendors would come at a further cost to you?
- Are outside vendors allowed?
- What level of personalization in decor is possible?

- What are your choices for food and drink (and flowers, cake, and the like)?
- Do they have in-house officiants? Can you use your own?
- Can you bring in your own photographer? Do they have suggested or required photographers?

FINDING NON-TRADITIONAL VENUES

There are so many places that you can get married that there is no reason to limit yourself to venues specifically marketed to weddings. If you're not quite sure what kind of venue is right for you, Alyssa Griffith of Rose Gold Events suggests that you "keep an open mind. Think about places you loved as a kid, trips you've taken with your partner, fun adventures, and the like. Weddings can happen almost anywhere."

Instead of taking to the Internet to search specifically in wedding-venue directories, you might want to start searching generally for weddings that have taken place in your area. This might just give you new ideas (maybe you never thought of hosting a dinner-party wedding in your own home), and it may give you very specific leads. Alyssa says, "Maybe you'll find someone who was married at a private estate you never would have found otherwise. Or Yelp will pop up with a family-owned property or an art gallery that rents their space."

DESTINATION WEDDINGS

There are two kinds of destination weddings. The first is the wedding that you and your partner travel to but which is local to some of your family and friends. (Think: getting married in your hometown.) This tends to be somewhat easier to plan. The second planning scenario is the true destination wedding in a location where neither you nor your loved ones live. Regardless of the kind of destination event you're having, if you're not getting married locally, you and your partner will generally need to be twice as decisive and organized, and you should realize you'll have only half the control.

With that in mind, Nicole Fredrichs of Playa Bliss Weddings, and Meg Hotchkiss of La Vie En Rose shared some tips to consider when planning from afar.

> **Take an honest and upfront accounting of budget—both your own and your guests'.** You're not going to be able to do competitive price shopping on every item, so make sure you know your limits up front. Keep the budgets of your loved ones in mind, and make sure you plan accordingly (and realistically). Also, if you need to pay for hotel and airfare for anyone close to you, add those costs in at the get-go.

> **Plan in advance.** Chances are good that your family and friends will need some time to plan if you're asking them to get to an exotic location. Send out save-the-dates as soon as you can.

> **Consider hiring a local planner.** No, you don't always need a wedding planner. Yes, a destination wedding might be a good time to utilize one. If you don't know the local vendors (or even speak the language), having someone who really understands how to throw a wedding in the area can be worth its weight in gold. If hiring someone to help is out of your budget, call planners where you will be getting married and see if you can pay (or politely ask) someone to give you a bit of time as a consultant.

> **Consider using an all-inclusive venue.** Planning a wedding from a thousand miles (or a country) away is not the time to go 110 percent DIY. Don't fool yourself into thinking that you can show up at an unknown destination, do all your own flowers, make your food from scratch, decorate beautifully on your own . . . and stay sane. The magic here is the location, not all the personally crafted details. If you can find a venue that will do most of the work for you, go for it.

> **Take a planning trip if you can.** Your planning trip won't be much of a vacation. Instead it's going to be an appointment-packed trip to get acquainted with as many vendors and venues as possible. Come prepared to write checks, sign contracts, and make rapid-fire decisions.

> **Think about bringing in a local (to you) vendor or two.** Almost all wedding photographers are dying to shoot a wedding in a cool location, so chances are good you can get someone with a style you love, and who speaks your language (literally and figuratively), to fly in for a decent price. In addition, if you have specific hair and makeup needs that might not be met by the local talent, you might want to chat with your hairdresser about flying her (or him) somewhere exotic for a weekend.

> **Research the legal requirements.** Did you know that some states in Mexico require a chest X-ray to get legally hitched? Make sure you know exactly what hoops you need to jump through if you're trying to make the thing legal.

> **What will the weather be like? Is it high season or low season? Are there local festivals or holidays happening?** It's not always sunny, even in paradise. There might be a huge festival the week of your wedding that you've never heard of. Make sure you know if you're booking your wedding during the windy/rainy/mosquito/busy/festive/slow season.

> **Plan how (and what) you're transporting.** Remember that everything that you're crafting or otherwise bringing from home has to get to the location somehow. That "somehow" is probably in a suitcase or in a box shipped in advance. Plan for decor items that can pack down tightly, and minimize what you need to bring.

> **Don't overplan people's time.** People are coming to your far-off wedding for two reasons—to spend time with you and to relax and explore the surroundings. Plan your wedding, and maybe a get-together the night before. Otherwise, allow downtime for people to spend time together (and apart).

·→· PRO TIP ·→·

Julia Henning of Wedgewood Wedding and Banquet Centers recommends that when looking at alternative venues, you ask the following questions: "How long has the venue been there? Who's running it?" She says, "I can't tell you how many times we've gotten calls from people whose venue flaked because they had permit issues or weren't a legit venue." If you find a non-traditional venue that you love but is new or less experienced, consider getting wedding insurance in case something goes wrong. (Wedding insurance covers you before the wedding in the event of, say, your venue closing down and walking off with your deposit. This is different than event insurance, which covers the day-of; see page 36.)

What Is (and Isn't) Included?

When looking at more non-traditional venues, your job is to ask hard questions about what exactly is, and isn't, included.

Allie Shane of Pop the Champagne says, "Many non-traditional venues do not have kitchen spaces. Make sure your caterer is very aware of what is provided and available. I've even seen venues not provide a single trash can, no broom in case something breaks, and no water. These things can be a big deal."

Once you've figured out what additional things you might need to procure (from table rentals to trash cans to additional staff), add these items to the overall price. Quirky venues can often appear to be very affordable. And though you can often nab a good deal on them, you want to get a solid idea of the overall cost of throwing your party in that space before you commit. And no matter how far off the beaten track your venue is, always, always get a written contract (see pages 49–50).

IDEAS FOR NON-TRADITIONAL WEDDING VENUES

> Beaches
> Public parks
> Forests
> Mountaintops
> Cliffs by the ocean
> Open fields
> Barns
> Backyards
> Inside your home (or your parents' home, or a friend's home…)
> Private homes
> Private estates
> Vacation rentals
> Restaurants
> Art galleries

> Art studios
> Any museum (particularly less mainstream museums)
> Kids' museums
> Church halls
> Public social halls
> Lofts
> Warehouses
> Big hotel suites
> Parking garages
> Parking lots
> Firehouses
> Schools
> Anywhere else you can imagine . . .

How to Throw a Wedding in a Non-Traditional Space

If you're throwing a wedding in a non-traditional space, it turns out there is a pretty consistent list of tasks that you should take care of to make sure your wedding doesn't get shut down by the police. That list is obvious to hip wedding planners who spend their careers working off the beaten track, but it's less clear to the rest of us. So, whether you're getting married on a beach or in your own backyard, here is your starter checklist.

- **Research permits.** If you're having a wedding in a public place or a residential neighborhood, you may need to get one (or more) permits through the city or county to make it legal. Many parks, beaches, and historical sites will require you to have a party permit for groups over a particular number. Some may require you to have a specific wedding permit. If you are intending to serve food, you may need a food permit, along with an alcohol permit (if serving alcohol is permitted). In addition, putting up structures (anything from tents to dance floors to lighting) may require additional permits.

- **Research parking.** What are the parking limitations where you're getting hitched? Can you borrow a neighbor's field as a parking lot? Can you recommend a nearby garage? Do you need to pay for a valet service? Can you shuttle people in, or suggest the use of public transportation? Make sure to include any parking expenses that you'll have to shoulder in your cost estimates.

- **Research noise ordinances.** If you're throwing your wedding in your own home or at an art gallery that's never hosted a wedding before, it's important that you research your local sound ordinances, and make sure you follow them.

- **Check with the neighbors.** Wherever you're getting hitched, it's important to be a good neighbor. If you're getting married at home, or in a barn, make sure the locals know what's going on. The best defense is a good offense. Possibly one with cookies.

- **Get event insurance.** If you're hosting a wedding in a traditional venue, you will probably be covered by their insurance. However, if you're getting married somewhere more unusual, it's likely you'll need to provide your own. Often, you can add a rider to your homeowner's or renter's insurance, or you can get a policy through an event insurance company. This will typically cover everything from personal liability (someone trips and falls and breaks a leg), to damage to the property (your guest knocks over a candle and the barn burns down), to alcohol liability (a teenager illegally drinks your booze, drives, and crashes the car). These policies are generally very affordable, and though you probably won't need one, a hundred bucks or so for a million dollars in liability insurance is a good deal. Party safe.

RENTALS

One of the little-discussed perks of using a traditional wedding venue or a full-service caterer is that they normally take care of the rentals for you. If you're not using a traditional venue or caterer, make sure you calculate the rentals you need in your costs. (Yes, the taco truck is super-cheap, but you need to include tables and chairs, and probably tablecloths, and some sort of serveware, disposable or otherwise.) You, or someone else involved with the wedding, need to arrange for rentals, rental setup, and rental takedown.

After reading this section, you might have the genius idea that you'll just buy everything! It must be cheaper, you won't have to deal with a rental company, and then you could keep it all after the fact. But, I'd caution you to think carefully before you choose that path. First, chances are good that you are not going to have much of a post-wedding need for, say, ten large tablecloths, or one hundred thrifted dishes. Second, the genius of a rental company is that they *take care of* all these items for you. The tablecloths show up pressed, the dishes get whisked away without being scrubbed, and you don't have to store any of it (before or after the wedding). These are very good things. Plus, the using and reusing of items is green, not to mention sensible. (For a basic list of rentals to consider, see page 186 in the Appendix.)

I spoke to Alyssa Griffith of Rose Gold Events and Jesse Tombs, senior event producer for Alison Events, and compiled their best tips for working with rental companies.

Finding a Rental Company

- In most areas, there will be a limited pool of rental companies. Compare online reviews and prices to figure out which ones seem like a good fit.
- The main difference between rental companies is often not the price but

the quality of the items. Look at reviews online to see if they suggest that the linens arrived stained and the plates arrived chipped. However, if you feel like you can't get a good sense of quality from online reviews, feel free to ask to visit their showroom and take a look yourself (keeping in mind that showrooms tend to be stocked with their *best*-quality items).

- If you don't have a planner orchestrating your whole wedding day, you want to go with as few rental companies as possible. Ideally, you want one. That way you're dealing with one pickup and drop-off time, and one team setting up.

- When contacting rental companies, it helps to be organized. Consider making a PDF document with the date, times, location, contact names, wedding details, when you need rentals delivered, when they need to be picked up, a list of exactly what you need, and if you need the rental company to do any setup. This PDF can then be sent off to a few companies for quotes.

- When talking to rental companies, besides making sure they'll work with you without a professional account, ask if they have a minimum order amount, what their delivery and setup fees are, and how they want their dishes returned. (The best answer is scraped, not rinsed or washed.)

ORDER LOTS OF GLASSWARE (AND OTHER RENTAL TIPS)

Keep in mind that once you've found a company to work with, you can rely on the professional rental salespeople to make sure you've come up with a comprehensive list of what you need. (You might forget you need spoons, but they probably won't.) That said, here are some tips to guide you when you order.

- Order the maximum amount you think you'll need. If 150 people are invited but you are only expecting that 110 will actually come to the wedding, order enough for 150, just in case. It's usually easy to downgrade your order, but if you need extra tables or linens at the last minute, they may all be booked (or out of your color). You generally don't need to finalize your order till at least two weeks before, so you can make your adjustments then.

- If you're going to upgrade, spend your money on nicer linens. The cheapest linens really do look the cheapest, so that's a good place to splurge. If you have limited money, don't worry about upgrading the plates and serveware. Once food is on them (which is more or less right away), no one will notice the difference.

- Get chairs that are comfortable. Some of the fanciest and most expensive chairs are downright painful to sit in.

- Order what feels like a lot of glasses. Some planners order two to three glasses per type per guest (for a total of five to six glasses per person). Glasses get left half drunk, and you'll need more. And more. And more.
- Order some extras of plates and utensils. You never know when some will end up chipped or broken or missing.
- Remember to review exactly what you're serving and make sure you're ordering appropriately. If you're serving cake, do you have cake plates and forks? If you're having a champagne toast, do you have champagne glasses?
- Triple-check the day, time, and location for both delivery and pickup on the final invoice. This is one place where mistakes are often made . . . and results can be minorly catastrophic.

·•· PRO TIP ·•·

Meg Hotchkiss of La Vie En Rose Events advises, "Never skimp on glassware—running out of clean glasses can really kill a party. Order extra place settings to account for breakage, and extra napkins, too. Finally, if you're doing a buffet, rent extra linens for the buffet table so the caterer can put clean linens on the table after dinner. No one wants to look at a food-stained tablecloth!"

TABLE AND LINEN SIZES

When you start dealing with rentals, the welter of options can feel overwhelming. To help you get past that freak-out, here is basic information about the most common table sizes and their accompanying linens. Keep in mind that a rental company can help you sort through what's best for you. (And remember, you almost never need to splurge on the expensive chairs.)

- 30-Inch Cocktail: These come in short and tall versions. The short one is 30 inches from the floor; the standing cocktail version is 42 inches from the floor. Respectively, they require a 96-inch round linen, and a 120- or 132-inch round linen.

- 36-Inch Cocktail: These come in short and tall versions. The short one is 30 inches from the floor; the standing cocktail version is 42 inches from the floor. Respectively, they require a 96-inch round linen, and a 120- or 132-inch round linen.

- 48-Inch Round (4-foot table): This comfortably sits up to four people. It's often used as a table just for the couple, or as a cake table. Requires a 120- or 132-inch round linen.

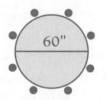

- 60-Inch Round (5-foot table): This comfortably seats eight people, and it can seat ten people. It requires a 108-inch round linen.

- 72-Inch Round (6-foot table): This comfortably seats ten people, and it can seat twelve. It requires a 132-inch round linen.

- 6-Foot Rectangle: This table is 6 feet long and 2-1/2 feet wide. It comfortably fits three people per long side. It requires a 90-inch by 132-inch linen or a 90-inch by 156-inch linen.

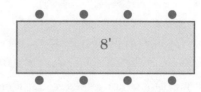

- 8-Foot Rectangle: This table is 8 feet long and 2-1/2 feet wide. It comfortably fits four people per long side. It requires a 90-inch by 156-inch linen.

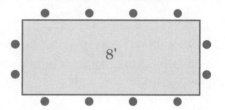

- King's Drape: This table is 8 feet long and 4 feet wide. It comfortably fits four people per side, plus two on each end. It's typically used as a buffet table, a bar, or seating for large groups. It requires a 108-inch by 156-inch linen.

RENTING A TENT

If you're having an outdoor wedding in an area or season that has a chance of rain, you need some sort of backup plan, and that backup plan is likely going to be a tent rental.

When picking where you're going to have your wedding, keep in mind that you really don't *want* to rent a tent if you don't have to. They are more expensive and more complicated than you'd think,

•→• PRO TIP •←•

Once you get into complexities like tent rentals, consider budgeting for a day-of coordinator (DOC) (see pages 56–58). It's important to know the realistic limits of what you can manage in a DIY fashion, and to know when to get help.

so that easy-breezy cheap outdoor venue might end up costing you much more than you're expecting.

Best Practices for Tent Rentals

- The first thing you want to know is what the tent companies' cancellation policies are, because chances are you'll want to cancel due to good weather. Because of that, a lot of companies make you pay a 50-percent non-refundable retainer up front, but find the best deal you can.
- If you're using a traditional wedding venue, ask what tent rental company they normally use.
- Consider what size tent you need. Use the information on table sizes (pages 38–39) and spacing (page 171) to figure out square footage needed. Your tent rental company should be able to help you with this.

- Consider what kind of tent you need. You're probably going with white, because anything else is stupid expensive. If it's winter, you'll need walls; if it's summer, you probably won't. You'll need to decide between a pole tent and a frame tent. In short, pole tents are cheaper and prettier, but they have to be staked into the ground. Frame tents will work on any surface.
- Do you need floors? If you're risking a hard rain that will turn the ground to mud, you might. Be advised, floors are damn expensive, so you may decide to skip them. That said, you'll probably want to rent at least enough flooring to create a dance floor.
- If you're going to be in the tent at night, you need lighting.
- If it's the winter, you're going to need heaters.
- When you get price quotes, make sure that delivery fees, labor and setup costs, accessories, fire and zoning permits, and breakdown are included.

But mostly, once you pick a tent rental company, defer to their expertise. No one is ever going to be an expert in wedding tents like an expert in wedding tents.

OTHER ITEMS YOU MIGHT NEED TO RENT

There are (unfortunately) some wedding locations where you're going to have to rent things like generators and port-a-potties. In these situations, it's a good idea to hire a day-of coordinator who knows his or her way around such things (see pages 56–58). Because even the most dedicated family and friends ever probably shouldn't be messing around with electricity and port-a-potties.

- **Generators:** If you're already going to be using an event rental company, see if you can find one that will also rent you generators. If not, they can often be rented through general equipment companies. You'll need to figure out what's going to be run off your generators to get guidance on how much power and how many generators you need. Also ask about sound. Although there are newer and quieter generators, you'll still want to position them far enough away from the main party so that you're not getting married to the sounds of a gentle mechanical hum.
- **Lighting:** The most common reason to rent lights for your wedding is because you actually need them (not for decorative reasons). It's possible that your reception hall only has fluorescent lighting, and you were going for something a little less . . . harsh. Or the space you rented just doesn't have bright enough lighting to be safe after dark. Or you're getting married in a field with no lighting at all. Whatever the situation is, if you're doing more than putting up a few strings of decorative lights, you need assistance from a professional. Lighting, and the requisite knowledge of power supply and rigging, is not something that falls in the "safe to DIY" category, unless you're an electrician. A general event rental company will typically be able to provide you with recommendations for a dedicated lighting company.
- **Amplification:** If your venue doesn't come equipped with basic AV equipment and you don't have a DJ or band to help you out, chances are good you will need to rent at least one microphone. Ceremonies with more than a handful of people and ceremonies outside should be miked. (You don't want people saying, "It seemed like a lovely ceremony . . . from what I could hear.") You might well need simple amplification for toasts as well. Sound rental companies have options for a DIY setup. Ask for wireless or lavalier mike options for more attractive and less obvious amplification.
- **Port-a-potties:** For obvious reasons, you'll need to find a dedicated port-a-potty company to handle this. These portable toilets run from plastic to marble, so you'll have your pick.

QUESTIONS TO ASK AT A VENUE WALK-THROUGH

"Venue walk-through" sounds like something you might do only with a high-end wedding planner, but it's really just the basic task of physically walking through a venue with a staff member and asking all those questions that a month before the wedding you'll realize you really care about.

Once you've gotten serious about a venue, it's smart to arrange a walk-through before you sign the contract. If you're having a destination wedding and can't do an in-person walk-through, arrange a time to talk to a staff member on the phone and pepper him or her with the same questions. You may also want to do a walk-through closer to the wedding, along with your day-of coordinator, wedding stage manager, or other helping hand, especially if you're using a non-traditional venue or one not used to hosting weddings.

Although you might not ask every question on this list, here is a comprehensive overview of issues that can be important from Katie Wannen of The Plannery.

> How many hours are included in the rental? Is it possible to add time to the rental, and if so, what is the cost? Keep in mind that two hours are generally needed for load-in, and one hour is generally needed for load-

out. For the sake of reference, the average venue rental is eight hours (usually divided up as two to three hours for load-in/load-out and five to six for the event). Daytime wedding slots are sometimes only six to seven hours, as the events tend to run shorter.

> Is it possible to have the ceremony rehearsal on site, and if so, is it included in the price? If so, how long is the rehearsal, when does it usually take place, and how far in advance can you book the time?

> Discuss load-in and load-out. Is there a loading dock? An elevator? Are there any loading restrictions? Ask if there are any specific difficulties or challenges at this venue. (Sometimes the building is old and has a tiny elevator, meaning load-in takes a lot longer. Sometimes there isn't an elevator at all, so the rental company will charge more to carry things up and down stairs.)

> If your wedding is during a cold or rainy season, do they have a built-in area for a coat check, or do they provide coat racks?

> Is a security guard required or recommended? Is one included in the rental fee, or is it an extra charge?

> If you have older guests or guests with disabilities, will they have any trouble entering and maneuvering around the facility? Is there an alternate entrance for those guests, if necessary?

> Is there a space for you and your wedding party to get ready on-site? If you're hav-

ing a Jewish wedding and need a spot for your *yichud*—the moment alone after the ceremony—do they have a way to accommodate that?

> What sort of lighting is included in the venue? Is it dimmable? (Note: Lighting is often forgotten because most site visits are made during the day, but weddings are often held at night.)

> What's the power like in the building? Vendors often pull a lot of electricity. Make sure you have a sense of whether outlets are scarce or if there's plenty of power to go around. It's also helpful to note where the outlets are located to help you later determine your layout—for instance, the photo booth can go in that corner, but only if they provide a ten-foot extension cord.

> Where are restrooms located? Are they easily accessible or do guests need to use stairs or an elevator to reach them? Are they wheelchair accessible?

> Where does the caterer set up? Some non-traditional venues that have been turned into wedding venues don't have a catering kitchen. Make sure you're okay with the location, setup, and logistics.

> Are there alcohol restrictions? Some venues don't allow red wine or dark liquor. Others require special permits. These permits will often be provided by the caterer, but check who normally provides them. Still others will allow you to provide your own alcohol as long as it's served by the caterer, whereas others won't allow it at all.

> Are there decor restrictions? Lots of venues don't allow confetti or other small items to be thrown. Others have open flame and candle restrictions, as well as sparkler restrictions. If these things matter to you (you were dying to do that sparkler exit) best to find out now and let that inform your final decision.

> Is the venue generally laid out in a specific way? Is there a recommended way to lay out the buffet, DJ, dance floor, and so on?

> Are there volume restrictions? Some venues, especially outdoor ones, have restrictions on what can and can't be played at certain hours and in certain spaces.

> Does the venue do more than one event on the same day? If the venue is large and has multiple spaces, or if it's a non-traditional space such as a theater, it's important to know what else, if anything, will be going on in the venue. Will you get the attention you need from the venue staff?

> Does the venue provide any equipment? Sometimes venues have tables and chairs available to clients, or A/V and lighting equipment. Ask the venue if they have an equipment inventory list that they can share or e-mail. (And ask to see what those chairs look like.)

> Is any additional event insurance required? (See page 36.)

> Are there rules about load-out? What are the guidelines for trash disposal?

When walking through a venue, Julia Henning of Wedgewood Wedding and Banquet Centers suggests, "Try to picture the flow of the day. Is there a place for you to get ready? How do your guests arrive, and where do they go?" She also points out that you should ask yourself if you like the people who work there. "Are they responsive? There are questions that arise throughout the planning process, so you want to work with someone who is responsive, pleasant, and helpful."

It's increasingly common to use the same venue for both your ceremony and your reception. In many cases, there will be two spaces: one where you get married (often outside), and one where you have the reception (often inside). If that is the case, consider who will strike the ceremony area after the ceremony bit is done (chairs will need to be put away, if you have a chuppah it will need to be taken down, etc.). However, in some venues, the same space will be used for both the ceremony and the reception. In that case the space will need to be "flipped" during the cocktail hour, which normally takes place in a smaller, ancillary location. If that's your situation, Katie Wannen of The Plannery advises that while looking at a potential venue, you should think about how the space fits the flow of your actual wedding and how your logistics will work. She says, "If you need to do a flip, how does that actually technically happen? Does it require anything extra that will cost money? Often it requires some rental drapes to hide things, and venues fail to mention that." If the space needs to be flipped, have a venue staff member walk you through the nitty-gritty of how that generally works.

Vendors, Friendors, and Doing It Yourself

4

THE FIRST STEP WHEN HIRING WEDding vendors is to figure out which ones, exactly, you need to hire. And by "need to hire," I obviously mean, "can afford to hire," because let's be real. The wedding industry tends to assume that you're hiring vendors for every single element of your wedding. If you can afford to do that, hooray! It's going to make your life significantly simpler. However, for most of us, hiring vendors is a process of figuring out what we care about the most, and what we can probably do on our own or just skip. The ratio of hire to DIY varies for every wedding, which is just how it should be.

HIRING VENDORS: WHO COMES FIRST?

When it comes to booking wedding vendors, you want to start with people who can reasonably only do one wedding a day (photographers, officiants, DJs, and the like). Next, you'll want to book vendors that traditionally can only do a limited number of weddings a day (say, caterers). Your final bookings should be lower-cost and lower-priority items, along with vendors that can service multiple weddings in one day (florists, cake bakers). That said, if you know there is one vendor you care more about than any other, forget general rules and book that one first.

HOW VENDOR PRICING WORKS

Although the wedding industry as a machine is a little . . . gross, individual wedding vendors can be as awesome as the industry can be awful. Wedding vendors are often creatives who make a living running small businesses. Most of them are working hard to make a reasonable living, and the best ones are bending over backward to make their clients' weddings awesome.

Because of this, it can be important to reframe our usual it's-cheap-because-the-workers-are-paid-minimum-wage-by-a-huge-corporation mindset and realize you're now working mostly with mom-and-pop shops. With independent vendors, prices for an individual service might seem high to you. However, when you calculate how much time that person will spend on your wedding, how many weddings a vendor can do in a year, and subtract overhead,

the annual income you get is usually not terrifically high.

This doesn't mean that you should go out and spend piles and piles of money you don't have on your wedding. But it does mean that it's good to respect a vendor's pricing, and reciprocally, find vendors that can respect your budget. If you have a

·•· PRO TIP ·•·

If you are considering trying to negotiate with a wedding vendor, be aware that you're working with a small business that has to pay the bills, and conduct any negotiation from a place of respect and understanding. Maddie Eisenhart, APW's digital director and former wedding photographer, says, "The key to negotiating with vendors is to understand that it's a negotiation. Asking someone to lower his or her prices, without anything in return is a favor. Make sure you have something to bargain with: fewer services, shorter hours, a partial service trade, etc." And realize that vendors have often crunched the numbers and are already offering the possible best rate they can. So don't be shocked if you can't get much of a discount, no matter what deal you offer up.

more limited budget, you should also factor in time for research. With a little work, you can track down vendors who are just getting started and may have more affordable rates because they haven't quit their day jobs yet. The quality might not be as good, and the delivery might not be as smooth, but you'll know you helped to get a business started (while getting your needs met), and that's an awesome thing.

WHERE ARE ALL THE AWESOME VENDORS HIDING?

Figuring out where to search for vendors can be even more confusing than choosing the vendor you'd like to hire. You'll want to start with word-of-mouth recommendations or use the Internet as word of mouth.

If you have friends who just got married and share your taste, that is a great place to start. Another excellent resource is an online wedding planning community that shares your point of view—be that visual taste or personal outlook on weddings. Many wedding websites and blogs have a directory that vendors can pay a fee to be listed on. These directories tend to be somewhat self-selecting and can result in vendors that fit a specific vision of what weddings can be. If you do happen to have a wedding planner (or have booked one or two vendors, or a venue that you like), ask for recommendations. Wedding pros tend

to have a good read on which other pros are talented and reliable.

One of the best tricks for finding affordable vendors is to look at the huge variety of "real weddings" featured online. Go to any wedding website you like and look at the weddings that took place in your region. Usually, these weddings will have credits listed at the end—a listing of the wedding professionals who worked on the wedding. This is a great way to find vendors without huge advertising budgets (caterers, florists, etc.), as well as a way to find major vendors (photographers, planners) who may be just starting out and not advertising anywhere yet. Similarly, if you're using a traditional wedding venue, a Google search should yield you plenty of weddings (with vendors listed) that were held in the same location.

DON'T FORGET TO VET YOUR VENDORS

No matter how fantastic your reference is for a particular vendor (your BFF used this day-of coordinator that you loved, and everything during the wedding seemed to go off without a hitch), it's still your job to do basic research and due diligence before booking someone. First, figure out if this vendor's work is a fit for you and your needs. Just because a caterer or officiant was perfect for your sister doesn't mean that this person will be right for you. Second, ascertain that this person has a solid professional reputation. Although you shouldn't stay up nights worrying about vendors running off with your deposit (particularly because you made sure your contract was solid, as covered on pages 49–50), one of the problems (and joys!) of the wedding industry is that it facilitates brand-new business owners setting up shop. That means that even though a photographer might be super-talented, she might not be the most adept at client relationships or might occasionally mishandle money.

If you follow some version of the following due diligence plan, you have done a better job than 95 percent of couples. (And yes, you will reap the benefits.)

Step 1: Spend time on vendors' websites. File this under obvious but important. Poke around in their portfolios, and also read what they have to say about themselves and their businesses. If at all possible, you want to hire someone whose creative work is a natural fit for what you're looking for. Hiring a florist and then asking her if she can design like another florist almost never ends well. It's stressful for everyone and best if you can avoid it entirely.

Beyond that, any business owners worth their salt have spent some time making sure that the text and messaging on their websites tell you a little something about them. For vendors that you're going to spend one-on-one time with on your wedding day, pay attention to how they describe their personalities, their attitudes toward their work, and even if they use gender-neutral language (provided that is something that matters to you). Make sure they feel like a good fit for you and your partner.

Step 2: Do independent research. Although you would never hire roofers to work on your house without checking a few of their online reviews—and probably calling a few references—people hire expensive wedding vendors all the time without jumping through the same basic hoops. Weddings are imbued with so much emotion that it's easy to think that if a person feels like an emotional fit for you, that's all that matters. But nobody is perfect, and it's important to figure out if this photographer tends to deliver work late, or is grumpy with clients, or shoots in an invasive way during the ceremony. None of those things needs to be a deal breaker, but you need to figure out how someone works, and if that's something you can deal with. Look up your vendor on major online review sites (Yelp and Wedding Wire are current industry standards), but know that wedding reviews tend to run on the glowing side. Unless a vendor truly and disastrously messes up, clients tend to not write anything other than four-star reviews for people who worked on their weddings. If you decide you might actually hire this person, specifically ask for a few recent clients to talk to, and ask them what the vendor's strengths and weaknesses are. In private, a past client will probably feel comfortable telling you that the food was good but the catering team was disorganized.

Step 3: Meet in person (or have a long chat on the phone). As someone who spends a lot of time working online, I can tell you that it's not uncommon to think that you really know what someone is like, until you meet in person and find out that the online personality doesn't line up with the offline personality. So while you want to spend time looking at a vendor's website, do not skip the part where you meet up for coffee or set up an in-depth online phone date. The best advice I can give you on these meetings is to listen to your gut. If someone engages in high-pressure sales tactics, makes offhand condescending comments, doesn't respect your wedding budget or what you're trying to pull off, or just doesn't seem at all excited about your particular wedding—pay attention to that. Also, note the vendor's level of professionalism. In my experience, vendors who seem to have it professionally together, normally do. And people who seem like disorganized emotional messes . . . usually are. At the end of the meeting, if you like the person, *ask for past clients to talk to*. Sending a few e-mails is the single best kind of research.

WEDDING VENDOR CONTRACTS

I consistently see the same scenario play out. A vendor presents a contract to a couple, and the couple views the contract as non-negotiable. If they want the vendor, they have to sign it. So they do. Then months later, they start complaining that a vendor used their photos for advertising without checking with them (it was in the contract), or that they didn't get a floral proposal back as quickly as they wanted it (it was in the contract). Because my general rule is that you are not allowed to complain about people following contracts that you willingly signed, let's talk about how to end up with contracts that actually work for you.

For more detailed information on what you want in a wedding contract, I talked to attorney Ali Noland.

- **Contracts require an offer, acceptance, and consideration.** Consideration means that both parties provide something (a service, money, etc.). Without consideration, you don't have a contract; you have a legally unenforceable gift.
- **Get it in writing.** Although the law recognizes many verbal contracts, good luck trying to prove what was said. Hiring a good friend to cater? Your relationship shouldn't preclude a written contract; you'll want to make formal agreements with friends and family as well.
- **Get modifications to the contract in writing.** If you ask the caterer to add twenty-five meals, get an e-mail (or even a screen shot of a text) confirming

that agreement, and put it with the contract.

- **Get a copy.** Get a copy of your contract and keep it safe. If you can't prove you had a contract, having a contract does you no good.
- **Be specific.** Did you and the wedding designer agree to white flowers, or did you agree to white tulips? If you put down "white flowers" in the contract and he or she shows up with bunches of baby's breath . . . well, the contractual obligation was met.
- **Check the cancellation policy.** Make sure any contract has a clear cancellation policy, spelling out what a cancellation would mean for both parties. This clause should be designed to protect both you and the vendor, in the event of the unexpected. Make sure the policy is clear and seems fair. (And remember, cancellation doesn't mean you don't have to pay for services already performed.)
- **Who's paying?** If your mom is paying for the venue, it's probably best for her to sign on the line. If you sign for it, be aware that you are on the hook for payment if she suddenly backs out.
- **Spell out when and how payments are going to be made.** How much is being paid up front? Is it a deposit (normally refundable) or a retainer (normally non-refundable)? When do you owe the rest? Can you pay by credit card, or is it cash only?

- **Don't sign away your rights.** Don't sign a contract that says you can only sue the vendors in New York if you are both located in California. Don't sign anything that says you won't hold the vendors liable if they screw up. Contracts are to protect you, so don't sign away the parts that let you do just that.
- **Document.** Save your receipts. If something goes wrong, take pictures, and contact the vendor in writing. If, God forbid, you have to go to court, you want to make sure you can prove exactly what went down.

WHAT TO DO IF SOMETHING GOES WRONG

Here is the part of the book I hope you never have to read: how to deal with a contract gone awry. First, contact the vendor right away, and provide a chance to fix the issue. (It's best if you can document this in writing, at least if the vendor refuses to solve the problem.)

If the two of you can't come to a solution, consider turning to your credit card company or bank as a first line of defense. If a vendor drastically violates a contract, you can often notify your financial institution, which will stop payment on charges already made. (This is a great reason to pay by credit card, even if you pay off the bill immediately.) Although someone can obviously fight a credit card company, if a vendor is aware of being in the wrong, he or she usually won't (or won't win).

However, if that doesn't work and the breach of contract is substantial enough that you're ready to take legal action, notify your vendor in writing that because of X breach, you are refusing further payment. Please keep in mind that if you refuse further payment, you may be the one dragged to court, so don't do this unless you're sure your documentation is all in order. Ali Noland says, "You may get angry phone calls or e-mails from the vendor, but be careful: anything you say could be used against you in court. Many of us try to smooth over conflict by apologizing or being self-deprecating. Don't do that! As soon as you make a comment like, 'I'm probably overreacting,' you can bet that it will be the vendor's Exhibit A when you get to court. Your best bet is to consult an attorney. Your second-best bet is to keep your mouth shut—don't say anything. You have already stated that there was a material breach and that you are refusing payment; nothing more needs to be discussed."

Note: Don't follow this course of action because of a minor breach. If one flower was not what you discussed, that's annoying but not worth the cost of a legal fight you probably won't win, nor is it worth screwing the vendor out of payment. However, feel free to negotiate on minor issues. If a delivery was made terrifically late, call the company and ask for a reduction on your delivery fees. After some firm words, you may get it.

HIRING A PHOTOGRAPHER

Hiring a wedding photographer is a little different from hiring almost any other vendor for your wedding. With most vendors it's enough for them to do a good job and be reasonably professional. Of course you want that, but you also need to keep in mind that you're going to spend the majority of the day with your wedding photographer or photography team. That means that it's important that you feel comfortable with them, but more than that, it's really nice if you *like* them. When you look back on your wedding, they'll be part of your memories.

That said, photography is as technical as it is artistic. So you want to find a photographer who you think is cool and makes work you like at a price point that you can afford, but there are other issues worth thinking about.

- **The lighting situation for your wedding.** The easiest wedding to shoot is a wedding in the daytime, with a ceremony under shade and with great natural light. If that applies to your wedding, you can probably hire anyone you want. If, however, you're getting married in a dark church or you're having an outdoor evening wedding reception, it's really important that you specifically look for a photographer who is skilled in those lighting environments. Don't assume that experience equals skill in low lighting. When looking at a photographer's portfolio, look for weddings shot in lighting environments similar to what you expect at your wedding. Ask how the photographer would handle your particular situation. (Some photographers use external lights for dark receptions; others may rely on a camera's ability to see well in the dark.) If you notice shots taken in dim lighting are all processed in black and white, that's a hint that the photographer may not be super-comfortable in darker situations.

- **Price and services.** When looking at someone's pricing, be careful to see what's included in the package you're looking at. Things like second shooters, additional hours, hi-res JPEGs, albums, and engagement sessions may be included in the price quote, or they might be extra. Also remember, things like albums and prints can always be ordered later when you're not facing the burden of paying for a wedding.

- **The photographer's style.** The general advice given is that you should pick a photographer based on style (photojournalism, classic, arty, etc.). But the more important question is simply, do you like the portfolio? Beyond that, do you feel comfortable with the way the photographer works? If photojournalism means there won't be a posed picture of your granny, that might not

work for you. Make sure the photographer's working style will be a fit within the real-life context of your wedding.

- **Post-processing.** A lot of the work in modern photography is done in post-processing. When you're looking at a photographer's work, it's helpful to know that images don't come out of the camera the way that you see them. If everything in the portfolio looks a little pink, or slightly yellow, or kind of moody, that is the photographer's post-processing style. Make sure that you pick someone whose processing style you like.

- **Look at a full wedding.** Once you've gotten a sense of a photographer's work, I'd strongly urge you to ask to see a full wedding. Some photographers produce twenty amazing images from every wedding, with the remaining eight hundred images a bit uninspired. Although I tend to think that five amazing photos of your wedding are all you'll use over time, it is important to make sure you're getting what you're paying for. A high-priced, experienced photographer should deliver consistently inspired work. A less-expensive photographer should deliver you a few great shots, along with an album full of nice images.

- **Delivery.** Once your wedding has happened, you're going to want to get your hands on your photos. Now is the time to figure out how that will happen. Get the photographer's average turnaround times for images. Delivery of the full gallery can range from a week to six months. (Important note: Faster isn't always better. Photographers who return photos right away might not do a great job editing. On the flip side, a lot of talented photographers who want to keep prices low shoot a lot of weddings during the high season. Taking more time to deliver images sometimes gives them the time to deliver you flawless work.) What rights will you have to use your photos? Will you get hi-res JPEGs (hint: you want those), or will you have to order prints through the photographer? What publication rights will your photographer have? (See page 102 for more on copyright and usage rights.) And finally, find out if you'll get access to your unprocessed images. Photographers generally request that you never publish unprocessed work, but styles change, and in twenty years, you might want them.

ALTERNATIVE METHODS FOR CAPTURING THE DAY

You've done the math, and you just can't afford a professional wedding photographer. Or hell, you just don't care to pay for one. Never fear! You have a couple of options, though they both require a bit of planning.

HIRE A NON-PRO

Call around to local art schools or universities, and find out if they have photography students who might be interested in shooting a wedding. Alternatively, ask around to see if anyone you know has a friend who's really into taking pictures with a fancy camera but isn't a professional. This sort of non-professional photographer will often be thrilled to shoot a wedding and will have cheaper rates. If you're going this route, keep in mind that your goal is simply to get solid documentation of the day without relying on friends and family. When working with a non-pro, keep these things in mind:

- **Clearly talk through your expectations.** Because this photographer isn't used to shooting weddings, let her know the particulars: If you want the photographer to be unobtrusive during the ceremony, or to take a lot of pictures of your guests during the reception, or to not wear jeans, make that clear.
- **Come up with a basic shot list.** Again, this isn't someone who knows all five hundred shots she normally gets at a wedding. Provide a rough list of what you're looking for, along with a list of the group photos you want. Assign a helper to guide the crowd during family photos, and schedule a little extra time for that.

- **Ask for RAW files.** We could get into a long discussion about the difference between RAW files and JPEGs, but the short version is, RAW files allow a lot more control over the images in post-production. You don't want to be stuck with the filter your hobbyist photographer put over your JPEGs, and RAW gives you the ability to edit the images however you see fit (or hire a pro to edit them).
- **And of course, sign a contract.** (For more, see pages 49–50.)

·✦· PRO TIP ·✦·

When working with a non-pro, APW digital director and former wedding photographer Maddie Eisenhart suggests, "If there's any extra room in your photography budget, think about offering to rent equipment for your photographer. Better equipment can go a long way toward helping entry-level photographers take better photos. A three-day rental for a professional-level setup can be as little as $200 and can give you the peace of mind that if something breaks during the wedding, your photographer will have a backup."

DIYing Your Photos with the Help of Family and Friends

If you just want some photos of your wedding and don't mind varied image quality, having loved ones take some photos will work just fine. However, it's imperative that you plan ahead. Wedding guests don't want to show up at a wedding to be surprised by the news that they're also serving as the wedding photographer . . . using their iPhone. Here are some tips and tricks to make this happen:

- **Count on a decent handful.** If you look back at your parents' or grandparents' wedding albums, chances are there are all of thirty photos in there, and that's enough. You know what the couple looked like on their wedding day, and you don't need to relive it moment by moment. If you're DIYing your wedding photography, set your bar for a handful of photos you want to keep, and be aware that you may need to sort through a few thousand not great photos to get them.
- **Divide and conquer.** It's not fair to ask the one person you know who's halfway good with a camera to capture the whole day . . . for free. Because that's called hiring a non-professional (see above) and you should pay that person. The goal here is to just make sure that there are a few shots of each

part of the day. Figure out which family and friends are interested in helping out, and assign them parts of the festivities as their special projects to manage. They may also take shots at other times, but as a guest it's good to know you can have some drinks at the end of the reception because you took your photos during cocktail hour.

- **Set up a formal way to collect pictures.** You can have a computer set up at the reception for people to upload to at the end of the night. You can set up an app that will nab all of those social media photos. You can send out an e-mail with an upload link when you get back from your honeymoon. Just make sure you have a plan (or two).
- **Crowdsource.** With a little research (technologies are always changing, so hit the Internet here, hard), you can figure out how to download copies of photos from social media sites, usually by having people mark them with a particular hashtag. These photos won't be the highest resolution, but they're still great to have.
- **Remember to make prints.** Just like with pro-photos, 2,000 digital photos are not going to do you (or your future kids/nieces and nephews/friends) any good. Sort through, find your favorites, and print them.

WHO IS GOING TO PLAN AND RUN THIS THING?

Putting together a wedding comes in two key parts. First, it has to be planned. Chances are that some combination of you, your partner, and your loved ones will do the bulk of the planning. (That's why you bought this book, right?) But you and your partner can't execute the event on the day-of while also, you know, getting married and enjoying yourselves. That means that you need to decide if you'd like to hire a pro to help on your wedding day, or if you want to ask a friend or loved one to help. Both have advantages and disadvantages (some financial and some organizational).

Although this book is designed to help you cover the basics of pulling this party together, on the day of the wedding you need somebody running the show, and that person should not be you. On your wedding day you have to be free to get married, with all the wild and unpredictable emotions that go with it. And you can't do that while simultaneously making sure the DJ is setting up in the right place, at least not without dissolving into a puddle of tears or having a quiet nervous breakdown.

HIRING A WEDDING PLANNER

The role of "wedding planner" is more or less what it sounds like. If you hire someone for this role, that person will work with you for months to help you actually plan this party. Planners' level of involvement in the process can range from helping you with key decisions to actually just planning (and even designing) the whole event with a little bit of guidance—and a large check—provided by you.

Because most people are not going to be hiring someone to plan the whole wedding *for* them (though, boy, does that sound nice), let's review a realistic list of tasks that planners are skilled at assisting with:

- Finding a venue
- Hiring vendors
- Sourcing rental items
- Buying or creating decor items
- Creating planning timelines
- Creating day-of timelines
- Creating floor plans
- Basically anything else covered in this book

You might want to hire a wedding planner if: you or your partner work sixty hours a week and simply don't have time to plan this thing; you're planning a wedding with a ton of moving parts; you have parents that are difficult enough that you want someone who's *not you* to manage them; or you want to have a wedding, but you simply have no interest in planning it.

You can afford to hire a wedding planner if: you can reserve roughly 10 percent of

your budget for the luxury of having help. Although most planners don't charge a percentage of your wedding budget but instead charge a flat rate based on the complexity of your wedding and the number of guests, you still need to have a reasonable amount of extra cash on hand to make hiring a planner a solid choice.

Hiring a Day-Of Coordinator

The most common way to hire professional planning help for your wedding is to hire a DOC. Even though it says "day-of" right in the job title, any DOC worth her salt is probably something a little more like a "month-of plus a little consulting when you get started" coordinator. The amount of work that a DOC will do varies, but usually, she'll go over your basic plans with you when you book her. (This is a great time to ask if she has venue leads that might be a fit for you or if she thinks your taco truck picnic party is logistically a good idea.) After that, unless you contact her with a question, you probably won't hear much from her till a month or two before your wedding, at which point she will step in and help you gather all the information about your wedding and whip it into (organized) shape.

Here are some tasks a DOC should help you with:

- Reviewing all vendor and venue details and contracts

- Creating a day-of timeline
- Coming with you for a venue walk-through (see pages 42–43)
- Confirming all vendors
- Running the rehearsal
- Managing the day of the wedding (including keeping your drunk aunt away from your difficult mother-in-law)

You might want to hire a DOC if: you think you can reasonably afford it. The truth is that all weddings (unless it's five people at the courthouse) need someone keeping an eye on logistics. You can always find a friend or loved one to ask (see "Wedding Stage Manager" on pages 58–59), but that means that you need to be very organized during the planning process. For many of us, having a friend help out is the only real option, but if you can find the funds to pay a professional, you probably won't regret it. (Note: If your wedding is complex and has a lot of moving parts, or a whole lot of rentals to be managed, you may actually *need* a DOC, and just need to find a way to budget for it, along with the generators and port-a-potties.)

VENUE OR CATERING MANAGERS

You may also be assigned a venue manager or a catering manager. Those people have specific jobs and will work to take care of the logistical aspects of the location and the food service. They can be very valuable

people to have working your wedding, but they are not working for you to oversee the whole day.

DO ALL OF YOUR WEDDINGS LOOK THE SAME? AND OTHER QUESTIONS TO ASK

As with any other person you're hiring to play a key role in your wedding, it's important that you do some research before you sign a check. Here are some additional questions that you might want to ask potential planners or DOCs.

- What are their general philosophies about weddings?

⟶ PRO TIP ⟵

If you're lucky enough to live in an area where there are local planners who offer hourly consultant rates, grab one of them for an hour or two of their best advice at the beginning of planning. They know the lay of the local land (vendors, venues, the works), and those two hours will save you a fortune, and your sanity, further down the line. Also see if you can book an appointment near the end of planning for help making sure your timeline and logistical plans are watertight.

- Do they have minimum budgets that they work with?
- What types of venues do they work in?
- Do they do design? (Do you care?)
- How do they deal with difficult family members?
- Do all their weddings look the same (and have exactly the same vendor list)?

WEDDING STAGE MANAGER— YOUR DIY WEDDING PLANNER

Reading wedding magazines and blogs can give the impression that every couple has a wedding planner or DOC doing the hard work, but that's far from true. Most people don't have a professional to help plan their weddings, simply because they can't afford it. That doesn't mean, however, that weddings without planners don't have to be . . . planned, or otherwise managed.

If you're not hiring a pro, try to find a friend (or family member who is not too directly involved in the day) who will be your point person. Maybe you swap favors and stage-manage each other's weddings. Maybe you just owe your friend a magnum of champagne after the day is over. But find someone dependable and organized, who's fine taking your planning notebook the night before, and your cell phone the day-of, and keeping everything on track.

It's vital that you try to be as organized as possible in the lead-up to the day. Use chapter 11 to make sure you've covered all your bases. Then sit down with your wed-

ding stage manager a week or so before the wedding to go over all of your planning documents, and review your goals for how the wedding should go and what you specifically need help with.

If you've clearly organized things in advance, your wedding stage manager will just have to make sure setup and takedown happen according to plan, nudge people in the right direction, and put out any small fires that pop up. But most important, having someone in this role will take the pressure off you, so you can just go get married already.

WHAT YOUR DOC (OR WEDDING STAGE MANAGER) DOES

> Acts as the point person on all logistical questions and the main interface with vendors
> Keeps, and is familiar with, a binder with all logistical documents, information, and phone numbers (see page 181) to answer questions and solve problems
> Makes sure staff or your family and friends have set up the space appropriately, and that it matches your floor plan (page 170), your seating chart (page 172), and what the staff has been contracted to do
> Wears a watch all day
> Doesn't get drunk
> Manages the timeline and flow of events, gently prompting people when they need to move to the next activity
> Makes sure the ceremony is set up
> Helps cue the processional

> Stays calm, keeps everyone else calm, and pretends to have the solution to a problem (even if the solution needs to be figured out really quickly)
> Knows where everything is—pens to sign the guest book, safety pins for the bustle, extra copies of the vows
> Pays vendors who need final payment or tip
> Manages breakdown and load-out—sober

HIRING AN OFFICIANT

In the past few years it has become so popular to have a friend and family member officiate a wedding that couples often assume this is the route they should take, without really considering other options. Unless you're 110 percent sure who's going to make it legal (be it your best friend or your priest), it's worth reviewing the variety of wedding officiants you can use. Whoever you pick, keep in mind that this person will set the tone for your ceremony, and you should feel comfortable asking plenty of questions and working closely with him or her.

THE FOUR BASIC TYPES OF WEDDING OFFICIANTS

- **Clergy:** If you're getting married in a house of worship or are otherwise having a religious ceremony, you'll most likely be working with a clergy member as your wedding officiant. The distinct advantage of working with clergy is that they are usually skilled and experienced at performing weddings. In addition, they will often provide you—or in fact require—religious-based premarital counseling, which can often be helpful. The downside is that clergy members usually have rules that govern the ceremonies they perform. With a religious wedding, you will likely not be writing the service from scratch, nor will you have unlimited options.

  If you're taking this route, and you don't have a regular house of worship, start looking for your wedding officiant early. Keep in mind that some clergy members will only perform weddings for members of their congregation, due to time limitations. Additionally, in many cases, you will need to be committed to the teachings of a religion.

  Weddings performed for members of a congregation are often done for free (or for a minimal fee), with a donation suggested. Weddings performed for non-members may have a somewhat more significant fee attached.

- **A judge or civil servant:** In most municipalities judges, retired judges, and other civil servants can perform marriages. If you get married at a city hall, a judge will likely solemnize your marriage. However, you can also hire a judge (or ask a judge you know) to make it legal wherever you decide to get hitched. While a few retired judges do so many weddings that it virtually becomes a small business for them, almost all judges have done this gig at least once or twice. Some of them might not be the most electric officiants, but they tend to lend an air of dignity to the whole affair.

- **Officiants for hire:** As states have gotten more lenient about who, exactly, can make a marriage legal, they've opened up loopholes for regular citizens to become wedding officiants. Many of them are "ordained" through an online church, such as the Universal Life Church, work for a flat fee, and usually work with you to create a personalized (often secular) ceremony. Keep in mind that this class of wedding vendor has no standardized training, and the skills required are somewhat open ended. Because of this, it's extra important for you to do your due diligence (see pages 47–49). If you can, watch videos of the officiants performing weddings to get a feel for their styles. Also, feel free to ask lots of questions, from what they typically wear when they perform weddings to their views on marriage equality.
- **Friends and family:** Within the last decade a loved one performing a wedding service has become the most popular form of wedding officiating. There is an obvious advantage to this practice: the person solemnizing your wedding knows

you and loves you. That said, this person probably hasn't officiated a ton of weddings, may or may not be entirely comfortable in the role of master of ceremonies, and won't be able to guide you in creating a service. If you're going this route, be sure the loved one you pick will be truly comfortable in the role. (See the checklist for amateur officiants on pages 151–152.) And please, don't skip a wedding rehearsal (see pages 176–177).

HIRING A DJ

Not everyone is looking for the same thing when they hire a DJ. Lots of people just want someone who can play some tunes, but others are serious music people, looking for a club-level party.

If you're just aiming for a pretty good DJ, start looking at online reviews and ask friends for word-of-mouth recommendations. Find someone you like in your price point, create a do-not-play list (if you care to), and enjoy the tunes.

However, if you're looking for a serious performance DJ, someone who reads a crowd and creates musical art, you might need to do a little more digging. Start by approaching DJs who work in clubs. They (sadly) are wildly underpaid, so they will often charge you way less than a wedding DJ would. Keep in mind, however, these DJs are not going to be fluent in "wedding." If you need to keep the music clean for a specific period of time, or you need breaks

•✦• PRO TIP •✦•

Michael Antonia of The Flashdance advises that if you're hiring a DJ on the basis of musical skills, you shouldn't hire anyone who doesn't have a lot of work you can examine, which can come in the form of mixtapes, videos, or live recordings. Just like you wouldn't hire a photographer without looking at a portfolio, you shouldn't hire a DJ without hearing a sample.

for announcements, tell your DJ. There are also a handful of high-end wedding DJs who are serious musical artists. They'll cost more but should provide you with the best of both worlds—kick-ass music, and an understanding of how weddings work.

DIY DJING

We've all heard it: you can't self-DJ a wedding and have an awesome dance party. Hell, we've all probably been to a self-DJed party where the music went down in flames. Luckily, there is a very specific formula for making the DIY dance party work.

- **Rent amplification.** In the history of time, there has never been a raging dance party with reasonably quiet music. If you're going to do this yourself, consider renting professional amplification equipment. When researching your rental, talk to local AV companies about what would work for a party sound system. Also, make sure that they are going to set the system up on delivery and show someone how to use it. Ideally, find a family member or friend or two who know how a simple sound system works, and ask them to keep an eye on things.

- **Set up a formal playlist.** It's tempting to think that you can bring a computer, plug it into a sound system, and turn on a Spotify playlist or a Pandora channel and just let it run. Well, no. That's a great way to handle cocktail hour, or any other time when you're just looking for ambient sound. But if you want a dance party, you need to put the same thought and care into your set that a DJ would. The basic idea is that you pump up the crowd, then turn it down a notch to let them rest, then pump them up harder, then turn it down, and continue building excitement this way until you reach the final fever pitch . . . and then close it out sweet and slow, if you'd like to.

- **Play songs people know.** You know when people rush a dance floor? When they hear the first strains of a song and yell, "OMG I LOVE THIS SONG," and are on the dance floor before they've figured out exactly what song it is. Stick with stuff people have heard of before, with a solid beat. You want songs that fall into the slow-song or fast-song categories, not the shuffle-y middle. And remember, the older crowd is going to be out in force for the early part of your set. Play some classics everyone will like early on, then work your way up to that old-school hip-hop after Nana has gone off to bed.

- **Cross-fade and don't play whole songs.** Nothing kills a dance party faster than dead air. If you just put a playlist together and run it, you'll get dead air after every single song. Add to that the fact that your average pop song is long. Once you have your playlist put together, use a program like iTunes to set up the songs to cross-fade into each other—and do so before that eight-minute song has run its course.

- **Make it dark (if you can).** If your wedding is at night, think about what you can do to make your dance floor a low-light environment. There is a reason clubs keep it dim—lower light frees us from our inhibitions.

- **Consider using DJ mixes.** There are plenty of amazing DJs out there who put out killer mixes online for free. It's not cheating to go DIYish and use them. (Just make sure you're complying with use policies.)

- **Put someone in charge.** You spend hours perfecting your playlist, and then you leave your sound system totally unattended. Someone decides to change a song and starts messing around with things. No go. Put someone in charge of making sure the music keeps flowing, and consider putting up a sign telling people not to touch the equipment.

- **Tell your friends you want a dance party.** If a crazy dance party is going to make the wedding for you, spread the word. People who love you will get out there, sober, on a well-lit DIY dance floor in the middle of the day if they know that's the one thing you want out of your wedding.

- **Nobody's gonna dance if you're not dancing.** If you want to make it a dance party, get out on the floor and start going for it. Nobody is going to leave a bride dancing by herself. If you're off chatting and mingling, people will take their cue from you.

HIRING A BAND

The question regularly posed in popular wedding media is, "Wedding band or DJ?" But for most of us, the equation is more, "Can I hire a professional or not?" If you've decided you can hire a pro, and you want to invest in a wedding band, you may have a good sense of what style of music you want, and who you want to hire. If you just know that you want live music, start getting serious about your research (both Internet and word of mouth). Just like DJs, you should expect that any bands worth their salt will have examples of their work online. You may also be able to see them in a live performance and get a feel for them that way.

If you're looking for musicians to just perform for a portion of your ceremony or reception (maybe you want live music as you go down the aisle), you can start with online research. However, this is also a great time to call local music schools or universities, and even local orchestras. There are always lots of musicians looking to make a few extra bucks, some more experienced (and hence more expensive) than others.

HIRING A HAIR STYLIST OR MAKEUP ARTIST

When it comes to hiring a hair stylist or makeup artist, word of mouth (and online reviews) go a long way. Your goal is to find someone skilled, reliable, and flexible. But more than that, it's best if you can find someone who makes you feel awesome about yourself, because you'll spend your getting-ready time with this person. I spoke to San Francisco hairstylist Yesenia Guinea for her tips on hiring a great stylist.

- **A free consultation, then a paid trial.** If you don't already know your stylist, you should make an appointment in the

salon (or meet for coffee) and have her spend ten minutes looking at your hair or face while you talk about your wedding. If you two feel like a fit, then you book a paid trial. If you don't, move on.
- **Find a price that makes you feel comfortable.** There are stylists at almost every price point, with the more expensive ones being more experienced. If an amount you're quoted doesn't work for you, keep looking (and remember that DIYing your hair and makeup is always an option).
- **Travel pricing.** If you need a stylist to come to you (early morning wedding, remote wedding, you'd just prefer it that way), expect to pay as much as double the normal in-salon price, plus mileage for the stylist. Instead of thinking of it as a markup, think of the in-salon price as a markdown, because the overhead and travel are otherwise taken care of.
- **The bride's hair and makeup is more expensive (but probably not for the reason you think).** If you're looking to get your ladies' hair and makeup done, expect the services for bridesmaids, moms, and other loved ones to be priced at about half what your hair and makeup costs. This is because the stylist is going to spend more time and take more care with you. On the day-of, she should tell you what she's doing each step of the way, letting you watch, ask questions, and suggest changes as needed.

YES, YOU CAN WIELD THE HAIRSPRAY YOURSELF

I always feel a little bit strange about the phrase "DIY hair and makeup," because it seems absurd that the act of getting yourself ready could be considered DIY. You probably have a reasonably good idea of how you like to look day-to-day, so if you're considering doing your own hair and makeup for your wedding, the goal is to figure out how to feel like the best-looking version of yourself.

Doing your own hair usually requires an extra set of hands but is otherwise reasonably straightforward. Figure out what kind of hairstyle you want, and find some Internet tutorials on how to do it well. (Hint: Don't pick something overly complex.) Ask a friend who's good with hair to help you out, and do a few test runs. Make sure you figure out what tools you'll need and bring it all to wherever you are getting ready. And let your friend off the perfection hook. Make it clear that you in no way expect perfect hair; you just want some help making your hair look pretty.

DIYING YOUR MAKEUP: YOUR REGULAR ROUTINE . . . PLUS

If you want to do your own makeup, there are a few extra tips and tricks that can make things go smoothly. I spoke to makeup artist Nikol Elaine about how best to approach the project, and I combined her smarts with what I've learned from a few years of product testing.

- Start by getting your skin in good condition, because great skin can make DIY makeup look nearly perfect. This can be as simple as keeping healthy and hydrated before the wedding. You can also give yourself a facial or even splurge on a professional facial a week or two before the day itself.
- Consider having your brows professionally done. Great brows make everything look close to flawless.
- Remember, no makeup is an option. If you don't regularly wear makeup and don't want to wear it on your wedding day, don't let anyone tell you that you "really should."
- Consider going to a makeup counter to get your makeup done. You can ask for help creating a wedding look and buy any makeup that seems helpful.
- Along those lines, consider treating yourself to a few nice makeup products. This might be just the time to upgrade your foundation. (And unlike paying for a stylist, you get to keep that fancy foundation after your wedding.)
- Keep it simple. Your wedding day is not the day to try applying false eyelashes for the first time. The goal is to do what you normally do, but bump it up a notch.
- Practice. You shouldn't be trying out your wedding makeup for the first time

on your wedding day. Do your makeup a few times beforehand, and take some pictures to see how it looks.

- If you're planning to wear makeup with SPF and are having a wedding where there will be flash photography, talk to your photographer and research SPF and flashback. You want to avoid the phenomenon of the SPF in your makeup reflecting light back, making you look like a ghost in pictures. Often, using a moisturizer with SPF with a non-SPF foundation on top of it will solve your problem, but do your research and flash test your foundation.

... AND EVERYONE ELSE

Of course, the number of people you can hire to help out at your wedding is nearly endless. Photo booth attendant? Bridal dresser? (Yes, that's a thing.) No matter who you're hiring, do your due diligence, use your common sense, and get a good contract.

TIPPING YOUR VENDORS

Vendor tips are often either forgotten from the budget till the last minute or way overthought. In reality, the guidelines are pretty simple (and low stress).

> The best wedding tip is always more business. If vendors have to pick between a lit-

tle extra cash and a great online review or word-of-mouth recommendation, they're going to pick the latter.

> Wedding tips are not done on percentages. You might tip 20 percent after a meal out, but 20 percent on your catering bill is a fortune. Instead, think of wedding tips as a little cash that your vendor wasn't expecting. Instead of going toward the company's bottom line, that $100 might go toward a nice night out.

> If the vendor owns the company, there is generally not the expectation that you'll tip. However, a little bit of cash, or a thoughtful gift, or a thank-you card for a job well done never goes amiss.

> If someone is an employee of a company, it's always nice to tip. If, say, your wedding planner works for a wedding-planning company, chances are that he or she is only making a fraction of what you're actually paying and would be beyond grateful for a tip.

> If you have waitstaff, custodians, or drivers, the nice thing to do is tip them—at least if they do a good job. Nothing crazy, but $20 each is always appreciated. You can set up a friend with an envelope full of $20 bills to pass out at the end of the night.

> And if someone goes way above and beyond for you, well, you know what to do. (Answer: All of the above. A good review, a thank-you card, and a nice tip.)

| SO YOU'VE BEEN READING THIS BOOK . . . AND DECIDED YOU WANT TO ELOPE |

AWESOME. MAY I PRESENT TO YOU THE EASIEST PLANNING LISTS EVER?

Just a Few Ways You Can Elope

- Just the two of you at city hall.
- Just the two of you and an officiant on a cliff overlooking the ocean or a mountaintop or a beach or, or, or . . .
- Just the two of you self-solemnizing your marriage in Colorado or D.C. (Currently the two localities in the US that allow self-solemnization, though several others offer a "self-uniting" marriage, with witnesses. Laws change over time, so do your research.)
- Both of you, and your closest family and friends, in whatever location you pick.
- Las Vegas. Just saying.

Marriage License: A Mini-Checklist

Every state and country has its own marriage license laws. They are too complex (and too constantly changing) to try to sum up here. Instead, remember to research the following if your elopement is going to involve a legal marriage license.

- What is the wait time between getting your license and the wedding?
- Do you need an appointment at city hall?
- What are the witness requirements? Who can serve as your witness?

Un-Plan Your Elopement

The best thing about elopements is that you *really* don't have to plan them. But here is a short list of things that you might want to do to fancy up your day. Feel free to gleefully ignore any or all of them.

- **Rings.** If you have them, remember them!
- **Vows.** Civil ceremonies conducted at the courthouse are short, but you are usually allowed to bring and read personal vows or traditional vows of your choice. (See pages 155–162.) If that appeals to you, write or otherwise select vows and remember to bring a printed copy.

- **Travel plans.** If you're getting married somewhere that's not local, make sure you book your tickets and make a hotel reservation. Consider treating yourself.

- **Your outfit.** I'm pretty sure this is what $100 lace mini-dresses were made for, but your taste in what you wear may vary.

- **An elopement photographer.** Many wedding photographers offer elopement rates that are way (way) under their regular wedding rates. Most elopement packages allow time for the ceremony and then for a mini-photo shoot afterward. If you want pro photos, Google "elopement photographer" and the location you're getting married in, or just call up local wedding photographers to see what they'd charge.

- **Flowers.** If you want to carry flowers, you can grab some from a local grocery store or call up a local flower shop and have them make you a quick bouquet. Otherwise, you can bring something to carry that's not floral or skip the whole thing.

- **Hair and makeup.** Just because you're eloping doesn't mean you can't get a blowout (or book full hair and makeup) if you feel like it. Or you can throw on lip balm and call it a day.

- **A plan to celebrate afterward.** You're going to be giddy and in love, and might want to go somewhere to eat and drink and celebrate, on your own or with your family. Consider making reservations, if you don't want to wing it.

- **Wedding announcements.** The traditional form is to send out something that looks a lot like a wedding invitation (sans RSVP card), announcing when and where you got hitched. Whether you send an e-mail or a letterpressed announcement, people want to hear the news.

- **Post-elopement party.** You can invite your nearest and dearest over for pizza and beer, or let your mom throw the wedding reception she always wanted. Or you can just say what's done is done (see: Wedding announcements, above).

 ## HOW TO RESCHEDULE OR CALL OFF YOUR WEDDING

IF YOU NEED TO RESCHEDULE YOUR WEDDING, OR EVEN CALL IT OFF, YOU'RE PROBABLY GOING THROUGH A difficult time. Maybe a family member is ill, or perhaps the two of you decided that getting hitched wasn't the way to go. Regardless, know that you're not the first or last people to go through this, and there's no shame in it.

Or, if you simply decided the big wedding you're planning is bullshit, and you're going to elope, then know that this next part is the necessary evil before the fun begins.

— continues —

Figuring out how to logistically handle canceling a large event, while also dealing with All the Feelings (your own and other people's), can be tough. I spoke to Alyssa Griffith of Rose Gold Events to come up with a simple checklist to guide you through the process.

- **Let your venue and all of your vendors know.** It's important to e-mail people (mark your e-mails as "urgent") so you have a paper trail. However, keep in mind that people only need to know the basic facts, and it's fine to keep your e-mails succinct. If you don't hear back from someone within forty-eight hours, then call. Check your contracts (see pages 49–50) to get an idea of what to expect. In most cases you'll lose your deposit, and in some cases you may owe additional money.
- **Be realistic.** Chances are, you're going to lose quite a bit of money on deposits and fees. No matter how difficult your situation, most of the small businesses you're working with can't afford to give you back non-refundable deposits. You can hope that people will be kind and helpful, but it's best to go into it understanding that you'll still need to honor your contractual obligations. If you're moving your wedding date up (or back), you might be able to get more in the way of compromises, assuming the vendor or venue is able to work with your new date.
- **Work quickly.** The best bet is to get it out of the way as fast as you can, because it's probably not going to be a ton of fun. But more practically, the faster you move, the more likely you are to get some money back.
- **Did you purchase wedding insurance?** If you bought wedding insurance (page 34), you just hit your payday. Contact the insurance company right away to see what they'll be able to cover for you.
- **Let your guests know.** The traditional way to inform guests that the wedding is off, or the date is moved, is by mail. If you take this route, a simple letter will suffice. But if, because of circumstances, that's simply not possible, send people a simple but formal e-mail. (And make sure you have someone call everyone who might not check his or her mail.)
- **Cancel the honeymoon.** Or, you know, take it with your best girlfriend and a lot of wine.
- **Return all those gifts** (and take down the registry).

And remember, ask for help. If you're in the position of needing to return mounds of wedding presents or trying to negotiate contract cancellations, possibly while crying, call in the troops. You do not need to do this all yourself.

Cheers! Feeding Everyone

5

1. Start with who you want to have at your wedding. Then figure out what you can afford to feed them.

2. The practice of serving a full, seated meal at weddings is pretty new. A generation or so ago, that was reserved for the wealthy. Which makes sense, once you run the numbers.

3. It's nice to give people something to eat and drink to celebrate your union. Cake and punch will do nicely, as will lobster and champagne.

4. Whatever you serve, make sure your guests know what to expect. No one likes to show up starving and be presented with only cake. Or to bring no cash to a cash bar.

5. Serve people on time. Serve people on time. Serve people on time. (And if you're not serving a meal, don't have your reception at a mealtime.)

ONE NEARLY UNIVERSAL WEDDING tradition is to serve some sort of food and beverage after the ceremony. While what you serve can vary from cake and punch to a multi-hour three-course meal, taking a moment to toast and celebrate with your guests has a long and joyous history. Unfortunately, deciding *what* to serve isn't always as carefree as actually eating it.

Choosing food and drink is one of the bigger decisions you'll make while wedding planning. It tends to drive your costs, so it's key to figure out early if what you can reasonably afford is a low-key picnic or a formal sit-down dinner. My best advice is simply this: figure out who you want to have at your wedding, and then figure out what you can afford to feed them.

THE MANY WAYS TO FEED YOUR GUESTS

Luckily, there are as many ways to host people at a wedding as there are weddings. Although these days formal seated dinner receptions are portrayed as the norm, their widespread popularity is relatively recent. The truly wealthy have long had huge wedding feasts, but for everyone else, morning receptions, cake and punch on the church lawn, and potluck dinners have a much longer history. So if you're going with a hosting style that seems outside of the box—consider yourself part of hundreds of years of tradition.

To get you started brainstorming, here are a variety of wedding food-service options. They vary widely in investment of time and funds, and this chapter will help you figure out what is going to be a fit for you.

- **The Full-Service Caterer:** Not only do they serve good food, they take a ton of the work of the logistics of party planning off your (proverbial) plate.
- **The Traditional Caterer Serving Less-Traditional Food:** You can hire full-service pros and have them make tacos, or piles of appetizers, or whatever you can dream up (and get them to agree to).
- **The Restaurant Wedding:** You can have a wedding in any restaurant that will agree to have you. If the location isn't used to doing weddings, this might take a little extra planning, but you won't have to worry about the food!
- **The Food Truck:** Hire professionals to roll up in their kitchen and make delicious food. Food trucks can serve your guests right from the truck counter or function more like portable commercial kitchens. Either way, the logistics (and tables) are on you.
- **The Potluck Wedding:** You'll know it if you've surrounded yourself with the kind of people who do potlucks. If you have, page 83 has tricks to make this kind of wedding go as smoothly as possible.
- **The Catering Hack:** Think of this as really smart shopping, plus re-plating. Or self-catering, without cooking.
- **The Self-Catered Wedding:** The real deal. The whole enchilada. Not for the faint of heart (or the non-cook).

HOW TO FIND A FULL-SERVICE CATERER

You don't want to put off finding a caterer forever, but you shouldn't attempt to book one until you've come up with a rough guest count, booked a venue (and thusly set a date), and set a general budget for food. Once you've checked those boxes, get Googling, researching, and talking to friends and family.

Unlike many other vendors (hello, over-saturated wedding photographer market), there are generally going to be a limited number of wedding caterers in your area in your price range (and that applies to all price ranges, from high to low). Once you figure out who they are, you'll want to narrow it down to those you're interested in. Then—assuming you have more than one choice—contact them to get a rough price quote and *set up a tasting*. With many wedding vendors, it's easy to get a feel for their portfolios through online research. But all the photos in the world aren't going to tell you how food tastes . . . or if it was served on time.

What Full-Service Caterers Do

Keep in mind that full-service caterers do a ton of things that we don't think about. They don't just cook, they also generally set up your tables and chairs, provide the waitstaff (and often bartenders), serve the food on time, clean up the dining area and kitchen, pack up the leftovers, and take away the garbage. When you're calculating the price of traditional catering versus less traditional options, make sure you remember that a caterer's bill includes a ton of things that you'll have to pay for on your own if you go a more DIY route. On that

note, you want to make sure you're hiring someone who will do all those tasks skillfully and on time.

WHAT TO LOOK FOR IN A TRADITIONAL CATERER

Which brings us to your caterer due diligence. Alyssa Griffith of Rose Gold Events suggests that you think about these questions when picking a caterer:

> - Do you like the food?
> - Is the catering manager competent?
> - Does the catering staff seem like they'll work to meet your needs on your wedding day?
> - Is the chef who cooked for your tasting the same person who will cook for your wedding?
> - Are they true full-service caterers? (Do they do bar, rentals, lighting, setup, teardown, cleanup, etc.?)
> - Are there additional fees, such as cake cutting, corkage, or service charges?
> - Can you provide your own alcohol? (And if you can, will they serve it? Would they cover that under their insurance?)
> - Do they offer cakes? And if you prefer, can you provide your own cake?
> - What is their backup plan if a chef gets sick, or there is another crisis?
> - Will they give you references of recent couples they've worked with?

THINK OUTSIDE THE BOX

A good caterer should be able to prepare many kinds of tasty food, from a Middle Eastern spread to a pancake breakfast. Less-traditional food choices can be delicious, and they also offer the potential benefit of cost saving. The farther you steer away from pricey protein options (like the admittedly delicious steak and lobster), the more you can bring prices down.

FOOD SERVICE OPTIONS

Although any caterer can and should walk you through a range of food and service options, here are the basic variations. Make sure you talk to your caterer about comparative costs, including rentals, service, and food, for any options you're interested in.

- **Seated Meal:** This is thought of as the most-traditional wedding option, and it can also be the most expensive. Because of that, a generation or two ago it was reserved only for weddings of the very wealthy—by which I mean, if you have to skip it, don't feel bad for a second. While be-suited waiters bring a certain charm to your event, they also greatly increase your staffing costs.
- **Family-Style Meal:** The family-style meal involves large platters of food being served to each table, and passed around, just like you would do at

Thanksgiving dinner. All told, this is often cheaper than a meal served by waiters, but it can be more expensive than a buffet. You'll still need a decent number of servers to make this happen, and you'll need more food.

- **Buffet Meal:** This can be the most affordable service option for serving a full meal. You still need a buffet to be staffed—someone needs to tidy it up and refresh the food as it runs out—but your staff-to-guest ratio is much lower. That said, your food costs could be higher (because nobody likes an empty-looking buffet), so talk to your caterer to figure out what service option will ultimately be most cost effective. If your wedding is large, make sure you have a good plan for crowd control. You'll generally need one buffet line minimum per one hundred people.
- **Brunch or Lunch:** Although morning weddings can be cost effective in a variety of ways, the lunch or brunch meal doesn't always save you the fortune that is sometimes promised. Lunch lets you skip the aforementioned lobster with fewer people noticing, and it will definitely lower your alcohol bill. But the food alone won't tend to save you enough to justify moving your wedding to earlier in the day.
- **Heavy Appetizers/Cocktail Hour:** Here, you skip the expensive main courses, skip the pricey servers, and go hog wild on what are essentially snacks. Just make

sure you have enough food to really fill people up (particularly if you're also going to booze them up) and let the mixing and mingling begin.

ACCOMMODATING FOOD RESTRICTIONS AND ALLERGIES

It's possible you have a pretty-much-eats-everything crowd coming to your wedding, in which case don't worry too much about how you serve your food. But if you know that you have a number of people with any variety of food restrictions—vegetarian, vegan, gluten free, Kosher, Halal, and so on—you'll want to think through your food presentation a bit more carefully.

Keep in mind that your guests are grown adults, and they have many years under their belts of figuring out how to fend for themselves at mealtimes. The trick is simply to be accommodating enough so it's easy for your guests to make their own smart choices. (You don't want to be the wedding where a guest is trying to explain what being a vegetarian *means* to a baffled waiter . . . true story.)

In that spirit, here are some basic tips and tricks to accommodate all types of eaters, while still serving food you love.

> If you're serving a seated meal, plan ahead. Request people's dietary restrictions on your RSVP card, and label their escort cards appropriately (see page 172). Although you might not be able to accommodate every food restriction in this format, it's helpful if you can cover the most common ones in your crowd—vegetarian, Halal, you name it.

> Buffets offer the easiest way for people to select a meal that works for them, with minimal pressure.

> When preparing a buffet, label dishes with what's included, so people don't have to ask.

> Try to prepare your buffet in a way that separates out potentially problematic elements. Put cheese on the side, to accommodate dairy-free and vegan folks. Serve pork meatballs separately, or offer vegetarian pasta sauce in addition to one with meat.

> Don't feel pressure to offer a vegetarian (or gluten-free, etc.) main dish, if you wouldn't otherwise do so. If you provide enough hearty and delicious sides, it's easy enough to create a meal from them. The goal is to give vegetarians more options than a plate of potatoes and salad.

Rest assured, your guests know how to take care of themselves. People who keep strict Kosher may bring their own meals. Vegans might bring their own snacks. But the more you allow people to make smart, informed choices from among your offerings, the happier they'll be. And please, if you know that one-third of your guests have a particular food restriction, make sure your menu reflects that.

Alcohol Service Options

If your bar is being run by your caterer, a dedicated bar-catering service, or a venue, there are a few different ways pricing can work. The costs of these kinds of service can vary quite a bit, so it's good to get a detailed sense of how you will be billed, and what the expected costs might be.

- **Hosted Bar by Consumption:** Here, the host (that's you) pays for each drink served. Because you'll typically be paying a per-drink cost, this can get pricey. (And yes, you'll be paying for all those dead soldiers.)
- **Hosted Bar by Bottle:** The host pays only for bottles opened, whether they were poured from or not. This often means you'll end up paying for plenty of unused booze, so ask if you can take home the opened bottles. In this situation, request that bartenders open as they go.
- **Hosted Bar per Person:** The host pays a flat amount for the duration of the party or for each hour. This tends to be a fair way to pay because the teetotalers in the crowd balance out the heavy drinkers. Best, you're paying a flat (and hence predictable) fee.
- **Cash Bar:** This can be as simple as having the guests pay the bartenders directly for drinks or providing guests with a certain number of pre-paid drink tickets, after which they are on their own. This is less common for weddings in the US. If you're doing this, make sure you let everyone know in advance that they should expect a cash bar, so they bring money.

STANDARD WEDDING BAR OPTIONS

When deciding on what kind of alcohol you're going to serve, it's smart to consider your taste preferences as a couple, along with what your guests like and will expect. In some areas of the country and social circles, weddings that serve only beer and wine are common. In others, hard alcohol is generally expected. You may know that your social group is going to expect something specific, such as vodka, tequila, or whiskey. The goal here is to cater your choices to your budget and taste, while trying to keep things celebratory for the people you love.

- > **The One-Beverage Option:** If you're having a wedding on a tiny budget, it's possible that you're just going to serve one thing, be it some form of bubbly or beer, or the classic: champagne punch.
- > **Wine and Beer Only:** This form of bar service is very common on the West Coast, and much less common on the East Coast. It has the advantage of being relatively simple to plan and can be more affordable . . . depending on your taste in wine.

> **Wine and Beer . . . Plus Signature Cocktails:** One way to split the difference is to offer one or two signature cocktails (which can be pre-mixed), along with a selection of wine and beer.

> **A Modified Full Bar:** If you're planning to DIY your bar—or just want to keep costs down—the best option is to offer a modified full bar. Here, you generally offer a few dark liquors, a few light liquors, a few mixers, and some beer and wine options.

> **A Full Bar:** If you want everything, plus complex cocktails, you'll need a professional bartending team.

RESTAURANT WEDDINGS

The restaurant weddings of our imaginations may run toward a full Saturday night buyout of a fancy place, which can get really expensive really fast. If you want to consider a wedding at a restaurant on a more limited budget, here are some things to consider:

- **Ask about partial buyouts and off-days.** If you don't feel the need to have the whole place to yourself, ask if an eatery will rent you part of the space, or if an afternoon or non-weekend evening might get you a lower price.
- **Look beyond the usual suspects.** You can have a great wedding at a hole-in-the-wall Chinese place, a cozy Italian

cafe, or your local Mexican dive, so consider everything. The sky (and your taste) is the limit. If you're not set on a full meal, remember to look at local cafes, coffee places, and even nightclubs.

- **How will the food be set up?** Particularly if you're going with a restaurant that doesn't regularly host large parties, make sure you walk through your serving options. Figure out if a buffet or a limited menu will be more appropriate (for you and for them).
- **Ask about billing options.** There are multiple ways that a restaurant can charge you: per head, by item, with a flat buyout fee, or with a food and beverage minimum. However they charge, it's important to get a sense of what the whole party is likely to cost. (Note: If you're paying a food and beverage minimum, pay careful attention to the menu you set, so you can aim to meet but not exceed that fee.)

WEDDING CAKES: FLOUR, BUTTER, SUGAR (AND CASH)

Just when you finally get the feeling that you've gotten your wedding catering under control—and that you may not even go broke feeding everyone—you realize there is one thing you still need to figure out. The cake. "No big deal," you think to yourself, "How expensive

continues —

can a wedding cake really be?" And then you start checking prices, and . . . WHY?

In short, traditional wedding cakes are expensive for a few reasons. First, the basic ingredients (milk, eggs, butter) have become increasingly pricey in recent years. Second, wedding cakes are time intensive. Even if you're not planning on a cake with a zillion handcrafted sugar roses, a serious baker can only make a few large cakes on any given day, and wedding cakes generally need to be prepared in the last days before the wedding. Plus, wedding-cake baking takes serious skill, and paying for talent and training is never cheap.

If you want, and can afford, a traditional wedding cake, find someone you like and trust, and realize you're probably not being ripped off. But if you can't afford an expensive cake, here are some good options.

Wedding Cake Hacks

> Ask a local (non-wedding) bakery if they'd be up for making a simple wedding cake. Often they're pleased to, and they will charge significantly less.
> Get a few cakes from your local grocery store. In general, the fancier the store, the tastier the cakes. You can put the cakes on cake stands and decorate them with flowers.
> Ask a local culinary school. Aspiring pastry chefs have to practice on someone, and it might as well be you.

> Have a friend DIY. Baking a wedding cake is a serious proposition, even if you go with something simple. But that doesn't mean that your best friend who's also a serious baker might not be into giving up part of her weekend to make a cake as her gift to you.
> Skip the cake, and have other desserts— but keep an eye on the budget. It turns out that other popular options, like pie, are not always cheaper than cake. You can always go with cheaper dessert options (candy! cookies!), but remember that even less-expensive options are pricey when you have to purchase them in bulk.
> Make dessert the potluck portion of the day. While a full potluck wedding (see pages 83–84) can be an undertaking, asking friends and family to bring dessert is a much-lower-key way to get people involved. Also, delicious.

NON-TRADITIONAL CATERING, FROM FOOD TRUCKS TO DIY

Wedding food doesn't have to come from a traditional wedding caterer, or even a professional restaurant kitchen. It can come in from food trucks, be catered in from a local restaurant, be purchased snacks and appetizers, or even be completely DIY.

However, if you're not using a full-service caterer, it's important to remember that all that service part is now going to be on you (or on a team of people you hire to help out). Every kind of non-traditional food service is going to have a similar checklist of items to take care of, from making sure tables and chairs are set up to making sure the garbage is taken away. It's important that you tally up additional costs (not to mention effort) before you commit to a particular kind of food service. Make sure that once the final numbers are run, this option still makes sense to you.

•→• PRO TIP •←•

If you're doing any form of semi-self-catering, San Francisco food writer Dana Eastland advises, "If you don't know about food safety, learn. There are online courses for certification that restaurants use for their staff, and they are about $20 per person. If you don't have someone you've hired or who loves you with a certification, I would highly recommend paying for someone to take the course and then put that person in charge of food safety. It's about an hour online and will bring up things that wouldn't even occur to you. And you'll sleep better."

THE DIY CATERING CHECKLIST

Here is a basic checklist for any wedding with non-traditional catering. Although the details will differ somewhat based on the type of food service you've picked, the basics will more or less stay the same.

> **Figure out what rentals you need.** These might include tables, chairs, plates, serving dishes, linens, flatware, and warmers. (For more see page 186.)
> **Figure if there is any serveware you want to purchase instead of rent.** It's generally not wise to purchase a set of one hundred china plates, so you might want to use compostables or disposables. If so, do your research and make your purchases.
> **Organize and figure out staffing.** How many people will you need to help out, and in what roles? Can you fill all of these slots with reliable family and friends? Do you need to hire additional help, whether local teenagers or professionals from a catering staffing company? (For more, see page 78.)
> **Create a detailed schedule.** Sadly, your meal will not set itself up, or take itself down. It's up to you to figure out exactly how this should happen (and how any dishes will get washed). (For more, see pages 85–87.)
> **If you're purchasing alcohol, figure out how much.** (For more, see page 80.)

continues

> **Figure out what event insurance you might need, particularly if you are serving alcohol.** (For more, see page 36.)
> **Figure out a food safety plan.** Ideally, ask someone to complete online food safety training and monitor food service on the day-of.
> **Figure out trash disposal.** Will you need to provide your own trash cans/garbage bags? Will you need to cart garbage away at the end of the night?

WHO'S TAKING OUT THE TRASH? AND OTHER STAFFING ISSUES

You will need people to help out with your food service, no matter how casual your wedding is. Allie Shane of Pop the Champagne says, "We do a ton of food truck and 'drop off' style weddings. One thing I hear quite commonly is, 'We are using all disposable plates and silverware, and people will just throw away their own trash.' No, they really won't." You'll need people on deck to help bus tables, cut the cake, empty trash cans, and clean up at the end of the night. Those people might be hired, or they might just be very dedicated family and friends. It's important that you review your staffing needs early (and factor in any additional costs).

If your wedding is of any serious size, it's wise to consider hiring a few helping hands to make things run more smoothly. You have two basic staffing options: you can hire from a staffing company, or you can hire local teenagers, friends, or other non-professionals. Here is the breakdown of how both options work.

- **A Professional Staffing Company:** There are companies out there that focus only on catering staffing. Although they are not going to be your cheapest option, they are trained to set up, serve, bus, bartend, and clean up. They are the "full-service" part of catering, without the catering. If you're planning on DIYing the food, hiring a few people from a staffing company should free you and your family up to completely enjoy the party. These companies also offer catering managers, and they are great if you have a lot of moving parts or more than two to three staff members. Otherwise, your wedding stage manager or wedding day-of coordinator should be able to cover it.
- **Non-Pros, Teenagers, and the Like:** Hiring non-professionals will, of course, be way cheaper than hiring people from a staffing company. That said, they will need a lot more guidance. This is a great solution for a small wedding without a lot of complicated components (think, a wedding in your living room). No matter how simple the wedding, make sure you've deputized someone to be in charge of the hired hands, to point them in the

right direction, check to make sure everything has been cleaned up at the end of the party, write them checks, thank them, and send them home.

How Much Food Do You Need?

If you don't have a seasoned pro making the decisions about exactly how much food all these wedding guests are going to eat, it's going to be incumbent on you to do some calculations. While there is no perfect formula for amounts of food, it's better to overbuy than underbuy. Nobody likes to end up hungry (and possibly drunk) at a party because the food has run out.

The following guidelines should help you make basic purchasing decisions, but know your crowd and consider things like time of day, venue, and location.

Appetizers per Hour per Person

- For appetizers that will be followed by a meal, 3 to 4 bites
- For appetizers that will not be followed by a meal, 5 to 10 bites
- For appetizers not followed by a meal at a mealtime, 8 to 10 bites

For Mains and Meals

- 6 to 8 ounces of protein per person
- 4 to 6 ounces of sides per person
- 1 cup of salad per person
- 1 to 2 rolls or servings of bread per person

For Desserts

- Cake or pie, 1 slice per person
- Cupcakes, 1.5 per person
- Mini-cupcakes, 4 per person
- Cookie or dessert bar, 2 or more pieces per person

·•· PRO TIP ·•·

As Kristy List, a pastry chef who self-catered her own wedding, says, deciding on amounts of food is "a guessing game. And for the most part, if you run out of one dish and make too much of another, people aren't going to be flipping over tables. They're just going to go along with it and eat what's available."

HOW TO BUY ALCOHOL FOR YOUR WEDDING

When it comes to picking your venue, it can be wise to pay attention to the alcohol policy. Many venues require that you use their bar or contract with a bar service. However, some venues will let you bring your own booze. If you are able to do this, you may well save yourself a fortune. (Although, please

— *continues* —

check on corkage fees. Paying corkage on every can of PBR that you open is not something you ever want to have happen to you.)

If you're lucky enough to be able to buy your own spirits, decide what you want to serve (see wedding bar options on page 74) and then calculate how much you want to buy.

How Much Alcohol Should You Buy?

The general rule is that you should allow for **one drink per person per hour,** though I've listed some standard modifications to this formula below. That said, obviously keep your personal guest list in mind when making calculations.

Servings per Alcohol Container:

> **Wine:** 4 glasses per 750 ml bottle
> **Liquor:** 18 servings per 750 ml bottle
> **Beer Keg:** 165 servings per full keg

A note about bubbly: While it is perfectly possible to toast with anything (even water), people often want to provide something special for the toasts. Dana Eastland, a food writer in San Francisco, advises the following: "Cava from Spain, Prosecco from Italy, and sparkling wine from other non-Champagne regions are delicious, and they are almost always a better deal than French Champagne. If you're going

to serve bubbles as a toasting-only option, you want about 4 to 5 ounces per person, per toast." That calculates to about five glasses in every bottle of bubbly, so buy accordingly. (And remember to rent Champagne glasses for your toast.)

Standard Modifications:

> **Daytime, Sunday, and Weekday Weddings:** People tend to drink less, so round down your calculations by a case.
> **Self-Serve Bars, Non-Pro Bartenders, and Mason Jars:** When left to their own devices, or the devices of that college student you hired to help out, people end up with huge pours. (Same if you're serving booze in mason jars or some other stylish but oversized container.) In these circumstances, round up.
> **Signature Cocktail:** If you're offering a signature cocktail or two, subtract an hour from your purchasing calculations, as that's generally what's consumed during cocktail hour.

DIY Bar Examples by the Numbers

Great! So you know how many servings you need, and how many servings come in each bottle. But how much of everything should you buy? Depends on what kind of bar you're having.

Beer and Wine Bar: The traditional ratios for a modified beer and wine bar are 75 percent wine, 25 percent beer. You might change this formula based on your crowd or location.

HOW MUCH OF EACH? BEER, WINE & LIQUOR RATIOS

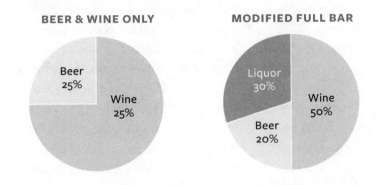

BEER & WINE ONLY

Beer 25%

Wine 25%

MODIFIED FULL BAR

Liquor 30%

Wine 50%

Beer 20%

EXAMPLE SCENARIO: 100 GUESTS, 6 HOURS, 600 SERVINGS
(that's 2 servings per person per hour)

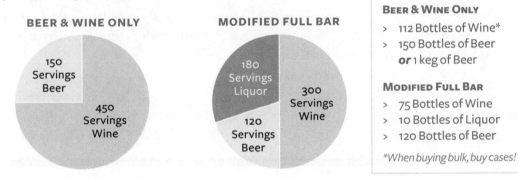

BEER & WINE ONLY

150 Servings Beer

450 Servings Wine

MODIFIED FULL BAR

180 Servings Liquor

300 Servings Wine

120 Servings Beer

> **WHAT YOU BUY**
>
> **BEER & WINE ONLY**
> > 112 Bottles of Wine*
> > 150 Bottles of Beer *or* 1 keg of Beer
>
> **MODIFIED FULL BAR**
> > 75 Bottles of Wine
> > 10 Bottles of Liquor
> > 120 Bottles of Beer
>
> **When buying bulk, buy cases!*

Modified Full Bar: The traditional ratios for a modified full bar are 50 percent wine, 20 percent beer, 30 percent liquor. Tailor your hard alcohol choices to your guest list, while making sure you can cover most basic drinks.

THE LEGALITIES:
LIABILITY INSURANCE AND DRAM LAWS

Now, for the less fun stuff. If you're providing your own alcohol, it's important to check if you'll be covered by your caterer's (or venue's) liability insurance. Although you won't know until you ask, generally you'll fall under a caterer's insurance if they are the ones serving the alcohol, but you won't if you have a self-serve bar. If you're not going to be otherwise insured, look into adding a rider to your homeowner's or renter's insurance, or getting a policy from a company specializing in event insurance (see page 36). Of course you don't want to think

— *continues* —

about what happens if someone driving home from your wedding crashes a car while drunk (or punches a hole through the venue's wall), but you really don't want to deal with getting sued and having no coverage.

Finally, make sure you look into liquor laws in your state and county. Dram laws tend to be odd, outdated relics and vary widely from place to place. If you can't buy booze on a Sunday or in a grocery store or return your leftovers, you'll want to know that in advance.

FOOD TRUCKS

There is a reason food-truck wedding catering has become so popular: it's really cheap. It's also hip, but at the end of the day, it's damn affordable. That said, it leaves a lot of logistical issues and costs up to you to figure out. So, before you settle on hiring your favorite local taco truck, it's important that you work through the details.

The Ideal Food-Truck Situations:

- A casual wedding that's not organized around a meal. In this instance, you hire one or more food trucks, and your guests can wander up and get food if they feel like it.
- A wedding where the food trucks function as a (hidden) commercial kitchen, and the food is served in a more traditional buffet style.

The Non-Ideal Food-Truck Situation:

- You hire a small number of food trucks for a large number of guests, with the hope of serving everyone an affordable meal right from the truck, all at one time. Your guests end up standing in a terrifically long line for their food and bolt it down alone at their table, with everyone else still standing in line (or long finished).

FOOD-TRUCK ISSUES TO CONSIDER

You want to end up with an awesome food-truck meal, so let's break down the best way to do this.

- **Timing:** Food trucks serve food fast, but they usually serve people one at a time. There is a reason food-truck lines are long at festivals. The general recommendation is one food truck to at least every seventy-five guests, but even then, plan on the fact that not all seventy-five guests will be eating at once.
- **The (Possible) Buffet Option:** Some food trucks offer a buffet option. If you can find a truck that does, it may solve some of your timing issues, though you still need to deal with possible rentals and logistics.
- **Space and Parking Limitations:** You'll need to check with your venue to make sure there is a place for the food truck to park, and make sure that spot isn't

logistically or visually problematic (you probably don't want to get married with a food-truck backdrop). Also, check to figure out if they will need any power hookups, or if they'll be using generators (and how loud those generators will be).

- **Weather:** Is there a chance your guests will be waiting in line for food in the boiling heat or pouring rain? (I trust you have not planned your outdoor food-truck wedding for ten feet of snow.)
- **What is provided and what isn't?** Usually, food trucks roll up and serve food on paper plates, and it's possible you want something more formal (or seated). Run through the DIY catering checklist on pages 77–78 to make sure you're covering everything from chairs to help clearing the tables. Factor all these costs into your total catering bill, and make sure a food truck is still a good idea before you proceed.

YES, YOU CAN HAVE A POTLUCK WEDDING

There are many reasons to do a potluck wedding, if you're up for a bit of serious organization and logistical planning. There is nothing that creates the same we're-all-in-this-together feel as a community meal, all while cutting down on your catering bill in a major way. So if your priority is people (possibly a lot of people) and not fancy food, the potluck wedding might be a great way to get it done. Hayley Tuller, who

threw a fancy church-supper potluck wedding, shared her best thoughts on planning a potluck without losing your mind.

- **Is your crowd a potluck crowd? Are they local?** The idea of a potluck is not a good fit for every crowd. If many people you know have a dish they always bring to a potluck, you're on the right track. If everyone is going to show up with a side dish hastily bought at the store, this might not be for you. Also, most of your guests have to be local to your wedding to pull this off. You can't expect people to fly across the country with a casserole dish precariously balanced on their knees.

·•·· PRO TIP ·•··

Hayley Tuller, who had what she calls a "Couture Potluck" at her wedding, messaged the formal nature of their wedding this way: "I used the social cues embedded in wedding etiquette to let our guests know that the event would be a formal one, but just one that happened to feature a potluck. This meant making some choices I would not have made otherwise in order get across the theme, like formal invitations and formal seating charts complete with hand-lettered escort cards."

- **Let people know what to expect.** This is one of the cardinal rules of keeping your guests happy, but if you're doing something a bit unusual like a potluck, this goes double. Communicate clearly what will be happening on the invitation, wedding website, and through word of mouth.

- **Let people opt in.** Not everyone is going to want to participate in a wedding potluck, and that's okay. In an ideal world you allow people to opt in to bringing a dish, and make it clear that food is not the cost of admission to the

wedding. (You might do this by having a different potluck response form from your regular RSVP response form.)

- **Communicate and organize.** There are many ways to organize a potluck, from asking the A–Fs to bring salads, to asking people to tell you what they're bringing and steering later contributors to what you need. However, make sure you come up with some sort of plan to make sure you have a well-rounded meal.

- **Anchor your meal with a main dish.** In order to avoid showing up at your potluck and thinking, "Lucky us, fifty-four salads!" you're going to need to do some pre-planning. But consider covering the real issue (will people leave hungry?) by providing a few mains.

- **Consider your style.** When we think "potluck" we often think informal: church dinner, picnic lunch, that sort of thing. But communal food does not necessitate a particular style.

CATERING HACK IDEAS

How do you serve food for a regular party? Quite often, it's simply smart buying and re-plating of food. Think of it as self-catering... without the cooking part. Here are some ways to make that happen, wedding style:

> **Sandwich Platters:** Everywhere from gourmet grocery stores to delis offer sand-

wich platter catering. Use this as the basis of your picnic wedding, or your casual lunchtime reception.

> **Cheese and Charcuterie Platters:** Get big wheels of cheese from your local Costco or cheese place, along with fancy meats from your local gourmet supermarket. Put them on platters with some crackers and fruit garnish, and voilà!

> **Dips and Spreads:** You can pre-make large quantities of dishes like hummus or other tasty dips and serve them nicely plated with bread or crackers.

> **Cake and Punch (or Champagne Punch!):** For many years, cake and punch on the church lawn was one of the classic wedding receptions. Not only does it have a long history, it's also quite tasty.

> **Dessert Party:** Think of this as cake and punch . . . but with a lot more cake, and also some chocolates. Desserts can range from pre-bought, to homemade, to potluck.

> **Pre-Made Frozen Appetizers:** Stores like Costco or Trader Joe's offer pretty good frozen appetizers, which just need to be warmed and nicely plated.

> **DIY Food Stations:** You can take simple foods like fondue, s'mores, or ice cream sundaes, and make them fun (and affordable) interactive food stations.

> **Takeout from a Favorite Restaurant:** If you have a local place you love that will do large take-out or catering orders, talk to them about providing (affordable) food for your wedding.

> **Mix and Match:** A food truck or two, plus plated frozen appetizers, DIY bar . . . the sky is the limit!

SELF-CATERING

There is, as they say, no such thing as a free lunch. Or a free wedding dinner, when it comes to that. And though self-catering can really decrease your food cost (note I said "can" decrease; it won't always decrease it, particularly if you don't plan like crazy), it's also going to drastically increase your labor, not to mention the amount of logistical planning you need to do.

When should you consider self-catering your wedding? When you have a small wedding (think: a dinner party). When you (or a loved one) love to cook. When you (or a loved one) is experienced at cooking for large groups. When you (or a loved one) is willing to devote a huge amount of time to pulling this project off. And when you have a lot of help.

What You Need to Self-Cater

When thinking about cooking for a wedding, the first thing that comes to mind is the food (obviously). But food costs can account for less than half of your overall self-catering budget, with equipment costs eating up the rest. So before you get planning, consider the basic resources that you'll need. You'll need to beg, borrow, rent, or buy the following:

- **Cooking Equipment:** Kitchen space, oven space, refrigerator and freezer space, cooking pots, pans, spoons, and other utensils, and more serveware than you'll think you'll need
- **Service Equipment:** Tables, chairs, linens, plates, cups, silverware, serving platters, and utensils (For anything you need to buy new, consider shopping at a restaurant supply store. It will be cheaper, and the items you buy will be designed for serving large groups.)
- **Labor:** A head cook, helper cooks, a day-of kitchen manager (who is not getting married), servers, a cleanup crew
- **Time:** Your time, your helper cooks' time, your servers' time, your cleanup crews' time (And plenty of it.)

MEAL PLANNING

The real truth about making food for a large group of people is that there is no one-size-fits-all, foolproof strategy. All that said, here are some things to think about as you start planning your menu.

- Consider your crowd (and their dietary restrictions). Do you have a lot of vegetarians? Folks that are dairy or gluten free? A particularly carnivorous bunch? Adventurous eaters or play-it-safers? Although it's fine to consider

your tastes as a couple, make sure that the bulk of the planning is done based on what your guests are actually going to eat. (If your crowd has dietary limits, print a detailed menu, or label dishes with what's in them. It will save you a lot of explaining.)
- How much food (and how much of each type of food) should you serve? (For more on the art of guesstimating amounts, see page 79.)
- How much can you prep in advance versus prep on the day-of? How much refrigerator and storage space do you have? What are the ovens and other kitchen facilities like in your venue?
- How much hot food versus cold food would you like to serve? Although hot food can make things seem fancier, remember that you'll need to have both help and an oven to warm things at the reception location, and some chafing dishes if you're serving buffet-style.
- How are you going to transport this food? (Try to only consider recipes that will hold and transport well.)

SELF-CATERING PLANNING DOCUMENTS YOU'LL NEED

For self-catering, it's important to make clear and detailed planning documents and to share them with everyone who will be helping. Although you might not need every one of these documents, here is a list of lists that you should consider making.

> Timeline, covering everything from shopping to preparation to cleanup
> Detailed, step-by-step preparation list
> Recipes for everything being made
> Shopping lists, divided by trip
> List of items to order (Amazon is your friend when you need to buy serveware in bulk, as are restaurant supply stores.)

> What to bring to the venue
> Day-of prep list for the venue, including an oven/fridge/stovetop plan
> Where things should go on the buffet table, and what serving utensils each dish requires
> A setup and cleanup plan
> A running list of all those small things you might otherwise forget—from ketchup, to coffee stirrers, to trash cans, to brooms

Getting Everyone to Show Up (and Have a Good Time)

6

THERE ARE MOMENTS DURING WEDding planning when you wonder: Why are we doing this again? Why are we spending so much time thinking about damn table rentals? And for the non-elopers among us, the answer is usually because we want to celebrate an important moment in our lives with loved ones. That means that when we're finally ready to invite the people we care about to participate in our wedding, it can feel exciting . . . and sometimes a little bit scary.

From save-the-dates, to invitations, to wedding websites, to registries, to all those extra parties that people may be offering, here are some strategies to manage (relatively) painless communications with guests.

SAVE-THE-DATES

Save-the-dates (sometimes referred to by the rather unfortunate acronym STDs) are relatively recent inventions in the world of weddings. As families and friends have gotten more geographically dispersed, weddings have become more of a destination event for many of the players. As such, it's become common to let people know that they should, well, save the date, six months to a year in advance.

This practice is not mandatory, but it should be employed when it seems like it will be genuinely helpful (or when you really just want an excuse for more pretty paper goods). Save-the-dates can be anything from letterpressed cards that match your invitation suite, to magnets, to e-mails.

Keep in mind that save-the-dates have a way of locking you into a guest list far in advance of the wedding. Many a person has run out of space for guests after they sent these notices . . . or worse, had a falling out with a save-the-date recipient. When this happens, etiquette doesn't have much of a life preserver to throw you—so proceed with some caution.

INVITATION WORDING AND ETIQUETTE

Although wedding invitations can come in as many forms as there are weddings, it's wise to only get so creative with them.

What's most important is simply that they go out decently in advance of the wedding (ideally six weeks or more) and convey some basic information. Who are you? What are you doing? When and where are you doing it?

Because of that, the tried-and-true structure of invitation wording can be a helpful starting point for figuring out your own (possibly innovative) phrasing. Here is a general outline of how the wedding invitation usually breaks down.

The Host Line: The first line of the invitation is where you list who's hosting the wedding. In times past, the bride's family always hosted (and paid for) the wedding. Thankfully, those days are done. Hosting the wedding is, in the end, a symbolic honor that you get to choose how to distribute. One, both, or all of your sets or singles of parents can be listed as hosts. You can host the wedding yourself, in which case the first two lines are reversed, "Toni and Jamie invite you to . . . " or the host line is omitted entirely. You can also make the host line more general: "Together with their families."

There are two issues worth noting here. First, no matter what anyone says in the course of guilting you, the host line on the wedding invitation isn't for sale; it's an honor that you should bestow in a way that makes you feel comfortable. Second, this particular honor is generally only used

TOGETHER WITH
THEIR FAMILIES

— Host Line

TONI QUINN ROBINSON-WILLIAMS

— Names

&

JAMIE LEE KIM

INVITE YOU TO JOIN THEM AT THE
CELEBRATION OF THEIR MARRIAGE

— Invitation Line
— Action Line

SATURDAY, THE SEVENTH OF JUNE
TWO THOUSAND FOURTEEN
AT HALF PAST FOUR IN THE AFTERNOON

— Information

THE PROSPECT PAVILION
409 OCEAN PARKWAY
BROOKLYN, NEW YORK

Dinner & Dancing to Follow

— Party Line

INVITATION DESIGN BY PRINTABLEPRESS.COM

for the living (because these people are, ostensibly, inviting you to a party). A common way to honor the dead is to list the deceased alongside the member of the couple's name, such as, "Renee Smith, daughter of Beth Smith."

The Invitation Line: This is where you actually invite people. "The honor of your presence" is traditionally used to denote a religious service, whereas "The pleasure of your company" is used to denote a secular one, though you can use any phrasing you want. Feel free to set the tone with anything from "Invite you to share their joy as . . . " to "Want you to come party with us when. . . ."

The Names: This line seems self-evident until you start thinking about the details. Whose name goes first? (That honor traditionally belongs to the bride, but what if there are two brides? Or two grooms? Or you just don't want to do it that way?) Will you list both last names, or one last name, or no last names? Will the names be on the same line or different lines? There are no right or wrong answers, but several good questions.

The Action Line: What are you inviting people to share in? Traditionally, with the bride's parents hosting, this line read something like, "At the marriage of their daughter," but your line might read, "At the celebration of their marriage," "As they

exchange vows of love and commitment," or "As they finally tie the knot."

The Information: This is the one line where I strongly advise you to stick to the basics, because you want people to actually come to this thing. Time, date, and location should all be listed (though the address does not have to be, assuming it's otherwise easy to find).

The Party Line: What's coming after the wedding? This is your spot to get celebratory, and also to give guests a solid idea of what to expect. If you're not serving a full meal, this would be a great place to say, "Cake, punch, and revelry to follow," or to inform them of a gap of time or location change, "Party to follow at 7 p.m. at The Mark Hopkins Hotel." You can also use this line to just get creative and set the tone for the celebration. "Wild celebration to follow," "Confetti and magic to follow," "Join us for an intimate dinner following."

A NOTE ON CHILD-FREE WEDDINGS

There is a lot of controversy surrounding child-free weddings. Is it *allowed* to not invite kids to your wedding? Is it *polite*? Well, of course it's allowed, and if you do it, I certainly hope you'll be polite. However, if you have a lot of parents (particularly parents of young children) on your guest list, be aware that not being able to bring the kids can make attending your wedding tricky and might result in a somewhat lower attendance rate. Assuming you want to make this as easy as you can on the parents in the crowd, let's talk best practices.

> **Let everyone know early. I know.** Technically, only the people listed on the envelope are invited. However, people often pop the envelope right in the trash without a second look. So if your wedding is adults only, make sure to communicate that early, clearly, and kindly. Send your friends with kids a direct e-mail with the scoop, or put some charming but obvious text on your wedding website. (I generally suggest refraining from putting some variant of NO KIDS ALLOWED on actual paper goods, as it's a mite off-putting.)

> **Be aware this will be harder for non-local guests with kids.** If you're local, not bringing your kids to a wedding probably just means booking a babysitter. If you're traveling, leaving kids at home or arranging for child care in an unfamiliar place can be difficult.

> **Provide child-care options.** If you have a non-local crowd, make things as easy as possible for them. Consider offering group child care at or near the wedding site. If you don't want to do that, provide a list of child-care options, so they're not stuck trying to find a babysitter through a concierge.

> **Consider an exception for (possibly nursing) mothers of newborns.** Parents of newborns (particularly nursing parents), tend not to be able to be separated from their wee offspring for very long. If you have

a BFF who will have just had a baby, make a teeny-tiny human exception. The other parents will understand why, and your girl-friend will get a chance to get out of the house, maybe even in a pretty outfit. (And on that note, there is nothing wrong with making occasional exceptions because it seems like the right thing to do.)

> **Don't have your wedding at the zoo.** A nighttime black-tie reception with no kids? Naturally. A daytime wedding at the local arcade? Well. The kids in the crowd will be understandably bummed that they can't attend. In short, it's easier to justify no-kids in an adult environment. Having a balloon party at the zoo that your little nephew can't come to? You owe him one.

> **And please, have babies at brunch.** Your friends traveled a long way to get to your wedding and arranged child care for the ceremony and reception. That means they really (really) love you. Show your mutual admiration by letting them bring the little one to any other events you're having.

THE GENTLY FEMINIST GUIDELINES FOR ADDRESSING WEDDING INVITATIONS

There is often much hand-wringing about how invitations are addressed. This is, of course, a lot of emotional energy to spend on an envelope that is going to very quickly find its way into the trash, but such is the nature of weddings. To help you out in one or more fraught conversations, here are the basic (reasonably feminist) rules.

> Use people's actual names. There is a mistaken idea floating around that if your wedding invitation is formal, you must use the "Mr. and Mrs. His-First His-Last" form of address . . . even if the wife in question hasn't taken her husband's last name. You don't. Address people by the names they use.

> If you can, address people in the forms they prefer. If you know your granny likes to get her mail addressed to "Mrs. His-First His-Last," well, that's her choice to make. Once you're married, you're going to be dealing with trying to get people to address you in the form you prefer, so follow the golden rule when you can.

> Traditionally, people with different last names are listed on different lines, though you don't need to stick to this convention.

> If children are invited, list them on the envelope. (Or on the inner envelope if you have one.)

> Use honorifics, or don't. Or use honorifics for people you suspect strongly would like to be addressed thusly, and skip them for your friends. But if you use honorifics, please attempt to use them properly!

- "Miss" and (the adorable) "Master" are appropriate terms of address for children.
- Once a woman is sufficiently grown, address her as "Ms." if unmarried (just like you would address a man as "Mr.").
- Married women who don't share their husbands' last names have the honorific of "Ms.," not "Mrs."
- Many married women who do share their husband's last name also use the honorific "Ms."
- "Dr." is a term that some people use socially, and some don't. You can use it or not, but if you use it, please use it for everyone who is a doctor, not just men. (Where that idea came from, I can't even fathom.)
- Widows should be addressed in the same form that they preferred when their partners were living, unless they've decided to change their form of address. If that's "Mrs. His-First His-Last," that remains the same.

> Realize you'll make some mistakes, particularly if you have a slew of friends who just got married and you can't remember what names they're now using. Try your best to figure out their current form of address (that's what social media is for), apologize when you make a mistake, and then let it go.

Ms. Jane King-Moore
Mr. Joan Moore

Ms. Joan Moore
Mr. John King
Master Gregory Moore,
Miss Emma Moore, Miss Cait Moore

John and Jane Moore

Mrs. and Dr. Jane and Joan King-Moore

Mrs. and Mrs. Jane and Joan King-Moore

Mrs. John Moore

Mr. and Ms. John and Jane Moore

Mr. and Dr. John and Jane Moore

·•· PRO TIP ·•·

When you start looking at all the possible paper goods you can order as part of your wedding stationery, your head might start spinning. Here is the short list of what you might reasonably want to consider: Save-the-dates (see page 90), an actual wedding invitation, an RSVP card (because nobody will respond without one), a card with general information like directions and your wedding website, and envelopes. On the day-of, you might opt for programs and table numbers, and maybe even thank-you cards, but until the invitations are out, don't even bother worrying about those.

·•· PRO TIP ·•·

Taryn Westberg, founder of Glö, an online invitation and RSVP service, advises: "Don't wait until three days before your catering numbers are due to start calling everyone in panic. Add some calendar invites to remind yourself when to send the first gentle reminder and when to start picking up the phone and dialing. Another sanity-saver is to build in some buffer for the unexpected yea or nay. Expect one or two guests to drop out at the last minute and one or two others to call at the last minute and ask whether they can still come. If you are mentally and logistically prepared for this to happen, it will be less stressful when it does!"

People Are Terrible at RSVPing (Help Them Help You)

The day of your RSVP deadline seems like it will be a joyful one. Your e-mail will be flooded with happy responses and maybe even carefully crafted little notes, right? Um. Probably not. People are generally horrible at RSVPing (on time, at all, you name it).

Beyond facing up to the fact that you and your partner (hopefully with the help of a parent or friend) are going to spend a week tracking down all of those missing RSVP responses, here are some tips for making the collection of RSVPs slightly less painful.

- **Provide RSVP options.** The more options you give people, the less time you'll spend chasing down non-responders. Although chances are good you'll provide paper response cards, it never hurts to also offer an online or e-mail option, as they are most likely to elicit fast and accurate replies.

- **Number your RSVP cards.** Lightly number all of your RSVP cards with the number that corresponds to the guest on your spreadsheet. You'd think people would include their names and return addresses, but not everyone will.
- **Ask for responses two weeks before you need them.** First, everyone's going to aim to put that response card in the mail on the day of (or week of) your deadline. Second, you need at least a week to track people down for answers.
- **Use pre-addressed pre-stamped RSVP cards.** Make. This. Easy.

THANK-YOU NOTES

There are books and websites that will offer you reams of etiquette advice on how to send thank-you notes. My suggestion: ignore it. Not because it's not helpful or technically correct (it is often both). But because it can be overwhelming, and the one rule you really need is this:

SEND THANK-YOU NOTES.

Send them on mismatched stationery. Send them late. Send them early. Send a short acknowledgment of the gift, or a long gushing letter of thanks. It doesn't matter, as long as you send them.

Who should you send them to? People who sent you a gift, folks who threw you a shower, friends who helped with a DIY project, family who helped set up your wedding. In short, send them to anyone who did you a kindness.

Get them in the mail. That's all that matters.

WHAT TO INCLUDE IN A WEDDING WEBSITE

Do you need a wedding website? No. Are you going to have a wedding website? Probably. Before you get started crafting a personalized journey of your love story for your carefully designed website, let's discuss what's useful to include and what's totally optional. Wedding guests go to your wedding website mostly to check your registry information. If it's the day of the wedding, they might also check for the location. That means a carefully crafted how-we-met story might not be widely read (though it still might be fun to write).

That said, here are some legitimately helpful things to include on your wedding website.

- A way to RSVP. If you offer an online RSVP option, you're less likely to be chasing *everyone* down for answers.
- Your registry information. Old-school etiquette implies that you shouldn't list

your registry information anywhere. New-school etiquette dictates that your wedding guests really want to be able to go online, find the registry, and click on it to shop. If you disappoint them, expect many complaints.

- Information on a hotel block, if you have one.
- Transportation options, if they seem appropriate. This may be transportation you're providing (see pages 174–176), or local cab companies to call if guests end up slightly intoxicated.
- Directions. Ninety percent of guests will check your wedding website in last-minute panic of "But wait, how do we get to that state park again?"
- The time and location of any additional events that everyone is invited to. (Keep private events private.)
- A rough idea of what to wear. People know how to dress themselves, so refrain from offering explicit instructions like "wear pink" or "women wear dresses." But when a guest is trying to decide between summer dress and cocktail dress, or heels and flats, it's really comforting to have an idea of what other guests might be wearing.
- What to expect. This is your place to let people know if you'll be serving dessert only (so they eat first), or if the ceremony will be on sand (so they wear appropriate shoes), or if it's a cash bar (so they bring cash).

HOTEL BLOCKS

First up, let me relieve you of the notion that you need to provide every last thing for your guests, from hotel rooms to transportation. Adults (which most of your guests are, or are attached to) are wonderfully skilled creatures, capable of making their own travel and transportation plans.

However! Hotel blocks can be a nice, and very convenient, thing to provide. They're a great way to encourage many of your guests to stay in the same location or guide people's travel choices in an unfamiliar area.

If you are looking to book a hotel block, here are the basics:

> There are two kinds of hotel blocks: closed (aka guaranteed) blocks, and open (aka courtesy) blocks. Chances are good that you want the latter.

> With a guaranteed block, you are, you guessed it, guaranteeing that those rooms will be paid, and that you will pay for them (in a percentage or in full) if they are not booked. This is called the attrition rate, and you do not want it in your contract if you can avoid it. Why might you go with this option? Closed blocks allow you to reserve more rooms, and that may be the only way to reserve rooms if every single room in town is going to be booked on those days.

> With a courtesy block, a hotel is reserving ten to twenty rooms for you, up to a cutoff date, at which point they will be released. Generally, this is the option you want.
> Don't expect a better deal. Although many hotels are happy to set aside twenty rooms for two nights, that's a small volume of business for them, and they may not give you a discounted rate.
> If you know you have guests with a wide range of budgets, you might want to offer a few options. That may mean providing hotel blocks at three differently priced hotels, or it may mean providing one hotel block with a few other hotel ideas.

REGISTRIES AREN'T ABOUT YOU, EXACTLY

With so many registry options, and so many purported etiquette rules, registry decisions can feel like a confusing maze of (guilty) choices. The most solid advice I can give you is that gifts on your wedding day are not *exactly* about you—they're about people expressing love for you. And as with all forms of love, you don't always get to choose the way it's expressed, but you can try to be grateful for it in whatever form it comes. (But also, you should probably get some form of a registry to help guide the expressions of love away from strange

> ### ·-·· PRO TIP ·-··
>
> APW's Maddie Eisenhart suggests making sure your wedding website informs people without instructing them. "Give people all the important details they need to make an informed decision about how to approach your wedding (the grass is going to be like quicksand, so it might not be friendly for high-heeled shoes) rather than telling people how they should approach your wedding (we're getting married outdoors, so no fancy shoes allowed). No matter how nicely you phrase it, or how helpful your intentions are, no one likes to be told what to do, especially older guests who have been going to weddings for longer than you've been alive."

handcrafted pottery platters and oddly shaped salt and pepper shakers.)

Along those lines, here are some quick thoughts to guide you through the madness.

• Register for things you want, and things that you think you'll use for a very long time. No matter what the salesperson tells you, you don't need one of everything. Or china, if you don't want china.

- It's fine to upgrade. If you have cheap plates from your college days that shatter when you look at them wrong, register for some durable everyday ware that will see you through to retirement.

- Register for items at a variety of price points. Your super-broke girlfriend might get you the $15 flour sifter, which is great because you'll think of her when you use it. But chances are good that some random friend of your parents, and maybe your granddad, want to buy you something expensive. Let them. Put a few things that feel pricey to you on your registry and be delighted if someone gets one for you.

- If a traditional one-store (or two-store) registry doesn't feel right to you, look at universal registries. These are online registries that let you register for items from a whole variety of stores, so you can get fine china and a tent.

- Alternative registries (like charity registries) are great, but you might want to consider having a small traditional registry on the side. I know, I know, you don't need plates and you want to raise money for your favorite cause. But there are some people who are going to give you a tangible gift whether you like it or not, and if you don't offer them some guidance, you're going to get . . . what you get. Probably with no gift receipt.

- Honeymoon registries can work well for honeymoons that are not directly after your wedding. If you're jump-ing on a plane the day after you get hitched, make sure you're not depending too heavily on that registry. My non-scientific estimate is that 90 percent of wedding guests buy their gifts the weekend of the wedding, so if your next-day Hawaiian honeymoon is depending on what people give you, there might not be enough to make the trip.

- The best I can tell you about cash registries is to know your crowd. If you know your family and friends are fine with giving cash, feel free to consider it, but you probably don't need a registry. Just put the word out with a few key family members and friends. If you do this (and don't register) chances are good that at least some folks will give you cash. And other folks will give you whatever gifts they picked out, and that's just going to be that.

A NOTE ON GIVING GIFTS

The wedding industry will happily lead you to believe that you need to buy thank-you gifts for everyone involved in your wedding. Bridesmaids? In it for the strand of pearls. Groomsman? Living for the flask. But in real life, people are contributing to your wedding because they love you, and the best you can do is show your gratitude and love in return. There are a handful of folks you might want to thank, or just offer something that's more about commemorating an important moment than presenting an expensive gift. They are:

> Members of your wedding party
> Your officiant (if a friend or family member)
> Your parents
> Your new spouse

To the extent that you choose to give these people gifts, remember that the most thoughtful thing you can give them is probably a note or a letter. That is something they'll treasure long after the flask has found its way to the junk bin. Other meaningful gifts can be framed photos, books, religious items, or other mementos that are less about money and more about remembering this moment in time.

As with all things wedding, focus on the feelings, and let the sense of financial obligation (and matching earrings) go.

SOCIAL MEDIA AND WEDDINGS

Once upon a time (like, a handful of years ago) the only privacy concern you might have had about your wedding was that someone might crash it. But these days, weddings come with your own personal team of paparazzi, snapping photos and sharing them on social media. That means it's wise to take a time-out to decide if you care how your wedding is shared on the Internet, and to make sure you and your partner are on the same page about it.

TO SHARE . . .

Assuming you're delighted to have your friends share their excitement for you in the form of an Instagram feed, set a wedding hashtag. Make sure it's not already in use on the sharing platform of your choice, and then let everyone know what it is by putting it on your website, on a sign, or leaving a note on the tables. The next morning you can wake up and relive the celebration through everyone else's eyes.

OR NOT TO SHARE . . .

But maybe you're not comfortable with the idea of your wedding photos being posted live on the Internet—where those friends you couldn't invite, your ex, and everyone else can see them. Or maybe you or your families are just naturally private. That's okay, too. It is perfectly polite to ask your guests to refrain from hashtagging, if only for an evening.

If you want to limit sharing on social networks, or want to personally choose how much you share, consider putting a sign up where guests can see it when they walk in. The sign can ask that people not share at all, or just avoid a particular kind of sharing. Realize that whatever you do, the system will be imperfect. People may well share things you didn't want shared, just out of habit. Asking people politely to take things down is not rude, and deciding you don't care enough to ask is fine, too.

IS THAT THE QUESTION?

Because we live in an age where everyone has a cell phone, and everyone is a (nearly constant) photographer, it's common for wedding ceremonies to turn into a sea of phones. This is increasingly becoming an issue for photographers. (Not only do a hundred phones make a bad photograph, but everyone stepping in front of the photographers trying to get their shots means they can miss big moments.) Beyond that, our addiction to devices can mean that your community gets focused on documenting your wedding instead of experiencing it.

However, it's not all or nothing when it comes to weddings and our multitude of electronic devices. It's common for couples to ask guests to put away their phones and cameras during the ceremony. (Think about it this way: a ceremony is a little like a religious service, and people are expected to refrain from selfies in church.) If you'd like people to put their phones away and take a much deserved time-out to be in the moment with you, do it. A firm and polite announcement from your officiant at the beginning of the ceremony usually does the trick.

WEDDING VENDORS AND IMAGE USAGE RIGHTS

It's not just your loved ones who might share your wedding photos. Because photographers almost always hold the copy-right on their images (they give you full license to use them personally, but usually not commercially), they generally retain the rights to publish your pictures, unless otherwise stated in your contract. That means photographers often share wedding photos everywhere from their blogs to major online publications, as a way to market their businesses. If you don't want your photos shared publicly, include that in your vendor contracts. (See pages 51–54 for more on hiring photographers.)

PARTY, PARTY, PARTIES!

You're throwing a wedding! Yay, and also oh my God it's a lot of work. So when people start to bring up all the other parties that can go along with the modern wedding, it can feel a tad overwhelming.

Other parties can include:

> Showers
> Engagement parties
> Bachelor/Bachelorette parties
> Rehearsal dinners
> Welcome dinners
> Morning-after brunches
> Post-elopement receptions
> And more . . .

Here is the first rule of other parties: they are strictly optional. More than that, they are often parties that can, and should, be hosted and planned by other people. Don't worry too much about an elaborate etiquette code. If you want to have a shower, tell your best friends or aunts, or whoever would be up for throwing it, and see if they're in.

That said, the related rule of other parties is that if someone else is hosting it, you have limited control. Yes, you probably should have veto power. (If your mom's best friend wants to host a shower on a boat and you get horrible seasickness, you can politely say "no thanks.") But beyond that, everything might not be done exactly as it would if you were doing it. But hey, you don't have to do the work or pay for it, so let's call that a win.

The general rules of these parties are simple.

> They're not mandatory—for you, or for anyone who might throw or attend one.

> You don't have to try to fit a particular mold. A shower can be co-ed. It can be in a bar. You can have an engagement pizza party. Just do something that fits you and makes the invitees comfortable.

> You might have more than one party: a shower from your friends; a shower from your co-workers; a shower from your mom. If you do, they may all be very different, depending on the group invited. Multiple parties are fine, but feel free to say no to offers when you're just . . . done.

> If you invite someone to an ancillary wedding party, that person should also be invited to the wedding. (Exception: parties thrown by your office or social group or club.)

> Don't require a huge financial commitment from people (or be hurt if they can't make the party if it requires a ticket to Vegas).

> Send thank-you notes.

In This Hot Outfit, I Thee Wed

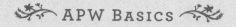

7

APW BASICS

1. Wear something on your wedding day that makes you feel like the best version of yourself. That can be a white dress or a custom suit or a feather skirt. Just do *you*.

2. You're not marrying the dress. Or even the pantsuit. It doesn't have to be "the one." You might not cry happy tears when you find it (or hell, even end up loving it).

3. It doesn't have to be white. Or a dress. Or from a bridal salon. There are plenty of ways to get a great wedding dress without ever stepping into a wedding dress store. Buy a dress from a major retailer. Buy a used dress. Buy a vintage dress. Buy a tux.

4. Shopping for traditional wedding dresses can be overwhelming and frustrating. That doesn't mean it's a scam. It does mean it's a confusing (and sometimes poorly run) industry. The more information you have on how it works, the better.

5. There is no reason that men and dapper ladies shouldn't spend as much time and energy on their outfits as any bride. I mean, let's be honest: which is going to get worn again? The dress with the layers of tulle or the sharp gray suit?

GREAT WEDDING OUTFITS—ONES that unabashedly reflect the personalities of the people wearing them—are hands down one of my favorite things. All the fantastic possibilities, from ball gowns, to long lace frocks, to feather capes, to sequined pantsuits, to impeccably tailored suits, are among the reasons I just can't quit weddings.

These outfits are not about spending a lot of money (at least not if you don't want to), or about pretending to be someone you're not. Instead they're just about being—for one kind of magical day—the shiniest version of yourself.

Of course, finding that awesome little number can be a tad tricky. And navigating the (often choppy) waters of the wedding and bridesmaid dress industry can take something of a primer on who, what, where, when, and OMG WHY?

To get you to your own sequined gown, sleek pantsuit, or dapper tux while keeping you sane and solvent, I'm going to break down why and how the wedding clothing industry works the way it does. This will give you the basic information you need to navigate it (or avoid it all together). I'll skip what seem like the staples of the literature—definitions of different wedding dress necklines and descriptions of all the beautiful and expensive fabrics that exist in the world. I figure you'll know what you like (and can afford) when you see it. The trick is to get you into the right store, the right online boutique, or just the right frame of mind.

WEDDING DRESSES: SCAM OR NOT?

After years of romantic movies, shows like *Say Yes to the Dress*, wedding magazines, and even TV commercials, it's easy to absorb a particular image of what finding a wedding dress will be like. TV tells us that we'll stand up on a pedestal in the center of a store and twirl around in a few beautiful dresses. Then at some point we find the *right* dress, and we burst into tears, as our moms beam and sniffle.

Record scratch.

It can be more than a little upsetting when we discover that wedding and bridesmaid dress shopping can be one of the most byzantine parts of wedding planning. Forget the ease of the information age; you can't even find the price of most dresses online. The wedding garment industry is still a complex world of policies and practices that make no sense to the uninitiated.

It would be easy to believe that much of the wedding dress industry is a scam, because it can be a serious pain in the ass. But as it turns out, it isn't . . . exactly. The problem is that many dress salons have a welter of poorly explained shop policies, and for years the business has thrived on asymmetrical information: they know what's going on; you're kept in the dark. Plus, it's hard to trust an industry that is built on the idea that it knows you better then you know you. (Yes! You want that beaded ball gown, no matter what you think!)

But when you get past all of those arguably bad business practices, the reality is that a traditional wedding dress is just *different* from almost any other clothing purchase you'll ever make. Wedding dresses are, by and large, made to order (which is different than custom), which means longer production timelines. They're also complex and relatively expensive items to produce, and they tend to need alterations when you finally get them. So, though the wedding dress industry might not be a scam, that knowledge doesn't make navigating it any easier without some guidance in the form of some altogether too-hard-to-find consumer information about wedding and bridesmaid dresses.

But because the point here is hot wedding outfits, not just layers of tulle by hook or by crook, it's also worth discussing buying a wedding dress in less-traditional ways—from department stores, to vintage, to used, to a dress ordered directly from China (okay, maybe don't do that). And since weddings are not just about dresses, we'll also discuss suiting, and other more dapper options.

On your wedding day, your outfits may look nothing like the ones you see on credit-card commercials. ("The perfect dress? Priceless.") But if you've found a look you love with minimal tears? Well, that's perfect enough.

TRADITIONAL WEDDING DRESSES

If you're aiming to get a dress that looks like what we traditionally think of as a wedding dress—white, structured, detailed, probably with a full skirt—chances are good you're going to be heading to a wedding dress salon. You might be hitting up big-box stores or you might be shopping at smaller boutiques, but in an ideal world, you'll find a store (and a shopping experience) that's a good fit for you.

How do you do that? Well, the first step is to just pick up the phone and call around. When you talk to salespeople, let them know your budget, your size, and an idea of what you want. You're looking for people who seem knowledgeable and friendly, and who are happy to help meet your needs, not pressure you into what they think you should have.

DRESSES BY THE DOLLARS

Whatever your budget, you can find a wedding dress, I swear to it. However, it's helpful to know what you can and should expect at various price points. I spoke to Jennifer Colgan, co-owner of the salon The Wedding Party, to get an overview of wedding dress pricing.

Under $500: The good news is that there are many more great options at this price point than ever before. These dresses will probably be polyester and have a simpler silhouette with less detailing.

Under $1,000: Dresses less than a grand will typically also be polyester. However, at this price point your dress will have an underskirt—the layers of fabric under the skirt that give a dress more structure and weight. That weight can be what gives a dress a really stunning fit.

— *continues* —

Under $2,000: When you move past the $1,000 mark, you'll start to see features like domestic production, better design, more layers of lining, head-to-toe lace, and a train. The complexity allowed by designs at this price point means that, as Jennifer says, "For some women, it's going to feel more like a 'traditional' wedding dress." However, this is also the price point where you start to see *less* traditional and edgier designs. In general, around $1,000, you start getting more design variety.

$2,000+: Once you head above $2,000, you'll see more intricate sewing and finishing. If you want expensive lace, fancy beading, head-to-toe feathers (just me?), silk, or work by an independent designer, chances are you'll be looking at a gown in this price range.

THE ALTERATIONS GAME

Although basic alterations to wedding and bridesmaid dresses make sense, a lot of common practices can seem like a ploy to run up the bill. Why do dresses come in sizes bigger than necessary? Why does it take so long to alter a dress?

Why most wedding dresses need alterations. It seems confusing that wedding dresses almost universally need alterations when dresses we buy off the rack don't. There are a few reasons for this. First, most of the clothing we wear day-to-day has some amount of stretch to it, which makes for very forgiving fit. Wedding dresses are, by and large, not made with fabrics with any give, meaning they'll usually need at least minor modifications to fit properly. Secondly, we don't expect a lot from day-to-day clothes, in part because we generally pay comparatively little for them. But with the investment and emotional importance of wedding dresses (not to mention the complexity of construction), we generally want to make sure they fit really well. Hence, alterations.

Wedding dress sizing and alterations. Because wedding dresses are not returnable, salons often order a size bigger than your normal size. This isn't always a bad plan, because taking in a bodice two inches isn't any more expensive than taking it in half an inch. However, if you're wearing a dress that you know fits, and you're confident that you're not going to put on much weight between now and the wedding, ask to order it in that size. You'll have to take personal responsibility for the results, but you'll save on needless alterations.

·►· PRO TIP ·◄·

If you're looking for a good seamstress or tailor, consider calling local wedding dress stores and asking for recommendations. Often they're happy to send business to people they work with regularly, no matter where you bought your dress.

What to look for in an alterations expert. Chances are you found a seamstress or tailor through your wedding dress salon, word of mouth, or online reviews. What should you expect?

- **A quote in advance.** Although a seamstress might be able to give you a ballpark quote on the phone, she'll generally need to see the dress in person to give you a more specific quote. But you should have an estimated quote before work starts.
- **A seamstress who listens to your needs and feelings about your dress.** As with all things wedding planning, don't work with anyone who doesn't listen to you in a respectful way.
- **Someone who doesn't rush you.** It's wise to move around in a gown, sit down in it, and see how it moves. Watch out for anyone who tries to move you along super quickly.

Alterations timelines. Some of the biggest fees you can pay a seamstress are rush fees. It's best to allow up to two months for most wedding dress alterations, but because reputable seamstresses often book up four to six months ahead of wedding season, lock them in when the dress order is placed.

Average alterations costs. When shopping for a wedding dress at a traditional salon, make sure your salesperson knows your *total* budget up front. That number should cover your dress *and* alterations. So if your budget is $1,000, and a salesperson trots out a dress for $950, make sure it fits like a glove. Otherwise, have a conversation about what alterations might cost, and make sure that works within your overall budget.

Although the cost of alterations will obviously vary dress by dress, region by region, year by year, here is a thumbnail sketch of what to expect.

- **$100–$400:** This will cover simple alterations, like a hem adjustment and bustle, or just a bodice taken in.
- **$300–$600:** This is probably the most common price range for wedding dress alterations. It can include hemming, bustling, or taking in the gown. More embellished and complex gowns will come in at the high end of this price range; simpler gowns will come in at the low end. If you're adding sleeves, expect a bigger bill.
- **$600–$1,000:** This range includes extensive reconstructions or major modifications for a mass-market wedding gown, or alterations to a couture gown.

Note that adding straps or buttons to a dress is generally very simple. Adding sleeves to a sleeveless (not strapless) dress is possible, but it requires patterning and will be more expensive. If you're hoping to change major things—the shape, the structure, or the design of a dress—there should

···•·· PRO TIP ··•···

If you buy a dress from a big-box store like David's Bridal, be aware that their in-house seamstress will often be limited by corporate policies. In general, dresses at these stores cannot be altered in a way that significantly changes the original style or silhouette. If you're looking for a massive overhaul of a gown from this store, you'll need to take it elsewhere. Or, you know, pick another dress.

be a good reason (like you're remaking your mama's gown); otherwise, it's probably just not the right dress for you.

Wedding Dress Timelines: Separating Fact from Fiction

More than a year before our wedding, I took an exploratory trip to a wedding dress salon. After about five minutes' browsing, a sales rep pulled me aside, asked for my wedding date, and told me, "Honey, you better pick a dress today, or you won't have it in time for the wedding." At the time, that claim seemed . . . false. And upon further research I can confirm that in almost all cases, wedding dresses simply do not take *that* long to order.

Although some stores will use falsely long timelines as a high-pressure sales technique, the truth of the matter is that traditional wedding dresses are not generally something you can buy off the rack. For a true no-stress wedding dress experience, you'll want to allow about six months for your dress to be delivered, and altered as needed. If you have a shorter time frame in mind, be honest with shops about your limitations, so they can pick dresses that can be produced more quickly or be rushed for a fee. If you're really in a hurry, try to find a salon with in-house alterations.

All that said, here are some general rules for various types of wedding dresses, and their associated timelines.

Mass-Produced Gowns: Some—though not many—manufacturers (particularly ones that sell online) have their wedding dress stock in a warehouse. If it's in stock, you should be able to have it in a week. If the dress is out of stock, you might wait six to eight weeks.

Cut-to-Order (Not Custom) Gowns: If you're buying a traditional wedding dress for under $2,000, chances are that your dress doesn't yet exist. When the order for your dress is placed, you're getting assigned a spot in the production line. The general turnaround on dresses like this is about three to six months.

Big-Box-Store Gowns: If you're shopping with a big wedding dress chain, dress delivery times are generally pretty fast.

Online ordering can get you a dress in two weeks (or less, if you pay rush shipping). Orders in store usually take six to twelve weeks. Note that for many big chains, plus-size dresses are not available online, meaning delivery takes a little longer. (Also note that some larger stores will sometimes have a limited inventory that you can buy off the rack.)

Couture Gowns: The gowns that really take forever are the ones made by hand. If you happen to be buying a truly couture wedding gown, then extend your time-line. Part of what you're paying for with a $20,000 dress is something that's hand-made just for you. And handmaking a dress takes time—sometimes many months.

BRIDAL ACCESSORIES: FROM SPARKLE TO BANGLE TO POUF

If you find a wedding dress you love in a wedding salon, your sales person may immediately steer you to the accessories section. Now that you've got the frothy confection, it's time to accessorize with any manner of white sparkly accessories . . . right? Well, maybe. Like much of the fashion world, the wedding business makes a significant chunk of its profits through heavily marked up accessories. And though you might find the perfect veil/crown/shoe/belt/miscellaneous sparkly thing in a bridal salon, remember that your wedding day accessories can be purchased anywhere, and they don't have to be expensive to look good.

When deciding what to spend, think about how big an impact a given accessory will have. If your dress is long, and your shoes won't be on display, you might want to pick something comfortable that you can wear again, instead of going with pricey brand-name "bridal" footwear. If you want a simple veil and you're only planning to wear it during the ceremony, consider finding something affordable online. (Or just make the thing. Veils are the world's simplest DIY.) But if you fall in love with the biggest, craziest, fashion-forward bridal tulle pouf for your head, and it's going to make the whole outfit? Girlfriend, go for it. Life is too short to second-guess those makes-your-heart-stop, this-is-your-chance accessories.

Body Image, Sizing, and Wedding Dresses

If you're not a perfect sample size—or are just not terrifically excited to stand on a podium and give people the chance to make comments about your body—wedding dress shopping can be a mite terrifying. I wish I could tell you that body shaming isn't an issue in wedding dress shopping. But of course that's not exactly true.

However, information is power, and a working knowledge of how the wedding dress sample-size system works should make you feel more equipped to navigate it. (Not to mention more empowered to deal firmly with anyone being impolite.)

Wedding dress sizing. When you start wedding dress shopping, chances are someone will tell you that the sizing is *crazy*. CRAZY. And it can be, but my best advice is this: ignore the sizes. The more expensive the dress, the more likely the size is based on vintage sizes, where a 12 is comparable to a modern size 4. More affordably priced dresses tend to have modern sizing. But the truth is, it genuinely does not matter what the number on your wedding dress is; it only matters that it fits in a way that looks amazing on you. Period.

Why Do Wedding Dresses Come in Such Limited Sample Sizes? Because wedding dresses are reasonably expensive and sold in somewhat limited quantities, wedding dress salons don't work like other clothing stores. Excepting some of the flagship big-box wedding dress stores, wedding salons can't possibly afford to stock every dress in every size. Instead, when they place their orders for the dresses that they're going to carry in a given year or season, they order one of each dress, in whatever size they figure is an average of their customers' sizes (for example, if their customers run the gamut between a size 2 and a 22, they'll probably carry a 10).

If you're smaller than the dress you try on, it's not much of an issue. You'll be clamped into the dress, and you'll get a good idea of what you'd look like in it. If you're a little bigger than the dress, you'll fit into it, even if it doesn't zip up. But if

you're more than a few sizes above the sample size, wedding dress shopping at salons can be amazingly frustrating. You obviously can't tell what you look like in a dress by standing *near* it.

HOW TO HAVE AN EMPOWERING WEDDING DRESS SHOPPING EXPERIENCE WHEN YOU WEAR A PLUS SIZE (OR ANY SIZE)

So what's a lady to do? Here are my best tips for empowering plus-size wedding dress shopping. (Though it's a must-read for any size.)

1. **Call Ahead.** Let the salon know what your size is, and ask them if they'll be able to work with you. Although they might not have sample sizes that are going to be the best fit, you're looking for someone who is informed, confident, and excited to be working with you.

2. **Big-Box Stores Are Your Friends.** Chain wedding dress stores get a bad rap, which they don't always deserve. But (bless them) their business model is based on having lots of dresses in the store. Whether or not you buy a dress, these stores are a great place to start seeing what looks good on you.

3. **It's Your Show.** We've all heard horror stories of salesladies who ask you if you're going to lose weight for your wedding, or who generally body shame you. Let's reframe: that's not just "how the wedding

industry is." Those are bad salespeople. If someone tries to shame you, nicely shut it down, and feel free to ask for a new salesperson (or leave). The people you encounter while wedding dress shopping are working for you. If they're doing a terrible job, take your dollars elsewhere.

4. **Go Custom (or Semi-Custom).** If you can't find something that works for you in a salon, consider getting something made. Getting a custom dress made means doing some research, but there are plenty of designers and seamstresses out there who excel in making plus-size wedding dresses. Also keep in mind that you don't always need to get a dress made from scratch. Tons of changes can be made to wedding dresses during the alteration phase: lots of sleeveless (not strapless) dresses can be altered post-production to add a sleeve; dresses can be shortened; and support can be added.

NOT ALL WEDDING DRESSES COME FROM WEDDING DRESS STORES

It's possible that reading about traditional wedding salons made you feel like you were breaking out in hives. Maybe you don't have months (or even weeks) to wait for your wedding dress. Maybe standing on a pedestal trying on wedding dresses is the stuff of your nightmares, not your dreams. If that's the case, let's discuss options!

MAJOR RETAILERS AND (NON-) WEDDING DRESSES

Buying an affordable (and possibly white) dress off the rack in a regular store is the dream, if you're not actually all that into traditional wedding dresses. If all goes well, this should net you an awesome dress for a fraction of the cost (with twice the sparkles, if sparkles are your thing).

As you're shopping, you may notice that white dresses are often slightly more expensive than non-white dresses and figure that the man is trying to get you down. The issue is more mundane: lining. White dresses need more lining to assure that onlookers won't be getting a direct look at your undergarments. That's worth $50.

Keep in mind that off-the-rack dresses usually have less-substantial lining and less-sophisticated built-in support than wedding dresses. Make sure you see the dress in bright light to confirm that it's not see-through, and be sure to move around in it to test how its structural integrity will stand up to activities like dancing. And remember, just because it's off the rack doesn't mean it might not need some tailoring.

BUYING AND SELLING USED DRESSES

There are several ways to buy a used wedding dress: online, from a consignment shop, and sometimes from a charity event.

⋆→⋅ PRO TIP ⋅→⋆

Maddie Eisenhart, APW's digital director and style editor, who spends much of her work life virtually shopping for dresses-that-really-should-be-worn-as-wedding-dresses-by-someone, offers the following advice, "In terms of purchasing, most retailers have major online and in-store sales during holiday periods, so you might as well wait until one of those take effect to buy. And if you specifically plan on buying off-the-rack and love glitter, wait until the winter. That's when you're most likely to see lots of glitzy evening gowns that could double as wedding dresses."

When shopping for a used dress, make sure you can live with whatever minor damage the dress might have. If you're buying online, see if there is a local store that carries the same dress you can try on in person first, and make sure the seller has a return policy.

Although buying a used wedding dress is a great idea, selling a used wedding dress is significantly harder, so don't bet your budget on it. There are a lot of things that can (and do) go wrong with this plan. Dresses get ripped or stained, rendering them un-salable. Yours just might not be a dress that sells well used, or it might not sell for the amount you were hoping for. Or, you might realize that you're really emotionally attached to your dress after the wedding and not want to sell it.

That said, there is nothing wrong with aiming to sell your dress, as long as you don't need guaranteed success for financial reasons. If your goal is to sell, plan ahead and think carefully about what kind of dress you buy.

- **Dresses That Sell Well:** Mid-range wedding dresses by popular designers that people really love but can't quite afford.
- **Dresses That Are Hard to Sell:** Super-affordable dresses (because people can afford them new), dresses by uncommon designers (because nobody is searching for them), dresses in unusual sizes (same), and expensive dresses (because if you're buying a $10,000 dress, you're probably not buying it used).

VINTAGE WEDDING DRESSES

There are three kinds of dresses that—more or less—fall under the rubric of vintage wedding dresses: authentic vintage wedding dresses, vintage party dresses, and custom re-creations or vintage reproductions. I spoke to Oran Scott of Relic Vintage in

San Francisco to get the best information on shopping vintage for your wedding.

- **Vintage Wedding Dresses:** True vintage wedding dresses can be stunning and fantastically priced, provided you can actually find one you fit into. Because they run small. Very small. Women historically married at much younger ages, corsets and other restrictive support garments were popular, and without modern nutrition, people were physically smaller. That means that vintage wedding dresses average modern sizes 2 to 4, aka tiny.
- **Vintage Party Dresses:** Vintage party dresses are a good, and more reasonably sized, option to consider. Like wedding dresses, these are often handmade and have fantastic detail and quality (they made it this long, after all). Non-wedding vintage tends to run up to modern sizes 18 to 20, providing lots more options.
- **Vintage Reproduction:** If you love vintage styling but just can't find a dress that works for you (or simply don't have the patience to dig around), you still have options. First up, consider vintage reproductions, which are often just as affordable as vintage (though they may lack the detail and quality). If you still can't find anything, you can look into having a custom vintage re-creation made for you.

THINGS TO KEEP IN MIND WHEN SHOPPING FOR A VINTAGE WEDDING DRESS

> Dresses tend to range from roughly $45 to $400.
> Budget for alterations with someone who knows vintage, along with possible minor restoration.
> Look for staining; spots on vintage fabric generally will not come out.
> If you feel the fabric pull apart as you try it on, the dress is no longer wearable.
> Remember that dresses can be taken in, or remade, but generally cannot be let out.
> Keep in mind that most vintage dresses were worn with pretty serious undergarments, ranging from waist cinchers to bullet bras. Expect to armor yourself with Spanx, at the very least, and possibly make alterations if you can't live with pointy boobs.

BUYING A DRESS FROM CHINA

Because you occasionally hear stories from people who ordered dresses from China and had everything go reasonably well, it's easy to harbor a secret hope that ordering directly from China means that you're ordering a lower-cost version of a designer dress, made in the same factory. Unfortunately, this is not the case. It's often unclear exactly who is making these dresses (though it is clear they are very poorly paid), but it's not the same factories churning mass-market wedding dresses, or even factories with any quality control to speak of. In short, there are better ways to snag a wedding dress for $200 or $300.

If you order a dress directly from China, here is what you *can* expect:

- Dress will generally be made from a cheap fabric.
- There will be far fewer layers in the skirt than in the original dress design.
- Detailing will be sub-par.
- Workmanship will generally be a little shoddy. This can range from not so bad (uneven hemlines), to downright terrible (unfinished uneven hemlines, pulling fabric, items hot-glued to the dress).
- To save on shipping costs, your dress will be turned inside out and shoved into an impossibly small envelope, so have a steamer ready.

But alright already! You're a woman of daring and risk, and you want to give this thing a whirl! Here is what you need to know to have the whole enterprise end in significantly fewer tears:

- Keep your expectations low. If your wedding dress is, in any serious sense, important to you, skip this plan. If your goal for your wedding dress is more

"Something white to get married in," things might turn out fine.

- Research, research, research. Make sure any store you order from has online reviews—lots of them. Although it's hard to find a direct-from-China dress shop that has all positive reviews (even the places you hear great things about seem to have horror stories), look for as many good reviews as possible.
- Make sure they have a money-back guarantee.
- Get your measurements taken. You can be measured by the person who does tailoring at your local dry cleaner; it just needs to be someone who knows what he or she is doing.
- That picture of the designer dress on the site is not what the company is selling (nor do they have the rights to use the photo). So ask if you can see photos of dresses that they've recently made, including detail shots.
- Consider asking for improvements. It may increase the cost, but it might be worth it to ask for more expensive fabrics (higher-thread-count poly; lace that's soft, not stiff), more layers on the skirt, and careful stitching.
- You can also ask for photos of the dress in progress, which might allow you to deal with errors in advance.
- And finally, allow extra time. The dress might not get to you as quickly as planned, and even if it does, it might not be exactly what you expected.

But hey, sometimes beauty comes from imperfection, and maybe a dress from China is exactly what the doctor ordered. (But seriously, maybe just buy a cheap dress on sale at a big-box store?)

THE PERFECT BRIDESMAID DRESS DOES NOT EXIST

Assuming you have attendants, figuring out what everyone is going to wear is a matter of balancing cost, practicality, and ease. You want everyone who's standing up for you to look and feel good, but you also want the process of picking outfits to not take over your (and your loved ones') life.

The trick is to figure out which, of a variety of options, is going to work best for you and your team. Do you want traditional bridesmaid dresses (matching or mismatching), rental bridesmaid dresses, off-the-rack outfits, or truly mismatched looks? (Or do you really not care, and will you opt out of the outfit game entirely?) Each plan has its advantages and disadvantages.

TRADITIONAL BRIDESMAID DRESSES

The advantages of traditional bridesmaid dresses are obvious. You can make one selection (of a specific style, or of a specific line of dresses), and everyone can get something that will look relatively cohesive without a lot of shopping or deliberating. Unfortunately, there are some

·✦· PRO TIP ·✦·

Corie Hardee, who owns Little Borrowed Dress, a rental bridesmaid-dress company, has some no-nonsense advice for picking attendant outfits. She says, "The perfect dress that everyone will like does not exist. When you give up on that idea, the guilt can fade and real solutions appear."

disadvantages as well, as anyone who has a bridesmaid dress shoved in the back of her closet knows.

First, let's just be honest: nobody is going to wear her bridesmaid dress again, no matter how cute it looks. Because flattering or not, it's identifiably a bridesmaid dress, now and forever.

Second, bridesmaid dresses are far more expensive than off-the-rack dresses, nearly impossible to try on in-store, and require far more alterations. Why is that? Well, unlike wedding dresses, of which designers usually produce a relatively limited line for each season, bridesmaid dresses are sold on the premise of sheer variety. You can get dresses in nearly any color, style, and size under the sun. That means that these dresses are not sitting, in all their infinite permutations, in a warehouse somewhere. Instead, they are made to order in somewhat small batches.

This results in dresses that are expensive because there is no economy of scale.

Unfortunately, they're also often somewhat ill fitting, as manufacturers have put their resources into coming up with a huge number of styles, not in patterning each style with great care. End result? Not only are the dresses pricey, but they show up needing lots of alterations.

Do the advantages outweigh the disadvantages? Only you and your ladies know. But I can tell you this. No matter what movies and media tell you, I—like most people I know—have never harbored any ill will for being asked to buy a traditional bridesmaid dress. Sometimes it was a little expensive. Sometimes it was a pain in the ass. But it always has been, in the final reckoning, worth the sacrifice. And though the dresses may have sat in my closet forever, I still think I look cute in the pictures.

When Your Bridesmaids Are All Across the Country . . .

If you've decided on traditional bridesmaid dresses, you now need to find a dress that all your people like (enough) and is flattering. Likely, you're trying to pull this off for a group of women scattered all over, because, let's be honest, you and your bridesmaids probably don't all live in one small town.

Here is how *not* to approach this project. Don't find a dress made by a particular designer on the Internet and tell all your

ladies to find a place to try it on. With the limited selection of dresses carried by salons, the odds of all your bridesmaids being able to try on the same dress in sizes near theirs are very slight.

The Big-Box Wedding Store Plan: These stores tend to carry many sizes and styles in bridesmaid dresses, so if you pick a dress carried by one of the big-box wedding megastores that have outposts everywhere, your ladies will have a much better chance finding it at locations near them. Let them get measured and try on the dress to make sure it's comfortable, but have them wait to buy. You'll want to place one order for the dresses, which often gets you a discount, and

---

·•· PRO TIP ·•·

No matter how you shop for bridesmaid dresses, Corie Hardee of Little Borrowed Dress reminds you to also have someone managing the logistics. She says, "Make sure that the dresses are actually ordered. Delegate your maid of honor or someone else to make sure the orders happen on time and are correct. Your people aren't going to tell you that they forgot or messed up or are worried about money, so delegate someone else to monitor all that."

always gets you dresses from the same dye lot, meaning the colors will match precisely.

The One-Salon Plan: Another easy option is to find a reputable local boutique that provides good one-on-one customer service. A salon like this will work with you and with your ladies remotely to find a dress or dresses that seem like they'll flatter everyone. They'll collect sizing information and organize ordering.

BRIDESMAID DRESS ALTERNATIVES

Thankfully, traditional bridesmaid dresses are not the only option available, though other choices involve a little more thinking outside the box, and often a bit more leg work.

- **Mismatched Bridesmaid Dresses:** It's become increasingly popular to have the ladies (and gents) standing up with you wear mismatched styles or colors that look chic together. (See pages 119–120 for more information on pulling it all together.)

- **Patterned Dresses:** The image of solid-colored bridesmaid dresses has been so burned into our minds that the idea of patterned dresses somehow seems surprising. But damn if it doesn't often look cute.

- **Off the Rack:** If you find a dress you like at a major retailer, remember it should come in a range of sizes and

be returnable. Make sure you or your bridesmaids are ready to purchase their dresses when you make your choice, because department stores and other major retailers change their inventory frequently. It would be easy to miss the purchase window.

- **Pants:** PANTS, right? Why is it so crazy to think of pants on bridesmaids? (More on women's suits on pages 120–121.)

- **Bridesmaid Separates:** If you want something that your ladies are much more likely to wear again, go with separates. Skirts (or pants) and tops can be paired and re-paired in a way that dresses can't.

- **Rental Dresses:** There are increasingly good options for rental bridesmaid dresses. This is brilliant, as it acknowledges that, yes, bridesmaids do want to look pretty, and no, they probably won't wear their dresses again. If you're interested in having your ladies wear traditional dresses (that they don't have to store in their closet afterward) for a good price, look into renting.

HOW TO MAKE MISMATCHED OUTFITS WORK

So you're skipping traditional wedding party gear and letting your people pick their own outfits. Great! Also, this tends to be not quite

— *continues* —

as easy as just saying, "Buy something nice in pink!" Most wedding parties want some level of guidance because (1) they are likely more invested in you being happy with their choices than with finding the elusive dress they would wear again, and (2) they want to coordinate enough to feel special.

Here are some guidelines for coming up with that lovely low-key mismatched look, while actually keeping everyone's stress levels low.

> Be honest with yourself about how much you care what your wedding party wears. Totally giving up control means some people might end up in something you think is ugly. If you're okay with that, skip this section and move on to your next project. Done and done! But if you want to have a more guided form of mismatch, read on.
> Start the planning process with pictures. Put together a board of images of outfits and outfit combos that you like. This will give your shoppers a clearer place to start than "bohemian rustic" or "just a long dress."
> From there, figure out a color palette. It's easier to create a cohesive look with variations of one color. If you're using a multitude of colors, it might be helpful to assign everyone a different hue.
> What are your general formality guidelines? No one wants to be the solo evening gown in a line of casual daytime dresses, so give people something to aim for.
> Consider exceptions to the rule. If you have one woman who only wears pants, or

a loved one with a markedly different body type then the rest of the crowd, or a lone guy (or heck, a lone girl), have a conversation to figure out how to come up with a look that makes that person feel comfortable, while still meshing with the other outfits.
> Consider a middle ground. It's possible to get bridesmaid dresses that come in one color, but in a whole variety of styles. (Or even get a range of, say, different colors of coral, in slightly different styles.) Narrowing the playing field in this way can actually make everyone feel *far* less stressed.

SUITS, SUITS, SUITS

The best advice for what grooms and dapper women should wear to their weddings is exactly the same as the advice for people who wear wedding dresses. Wear something that makes you feel like the best version of yourself. Break the rules you want to break, and to hell with the naysayers.

That said, suiting has its own complex logic, and it's always advisable to know the rules before you break them. Here is a rundown of how suits and other formalwear are bought and worn.

TYPES OF SUITS, OR WHAT TO DO WITH ALL THE BUTTONS

The first, and most baffling rule of suit wearing is that most suits have two buttons, and you only button one of them. Wedding planners tell me that one of their jobs on the day of the wedding is to explain that the second button of the suit shouldn't be buttoned (ever). For those of you who don't wear a suit to work every day, and won't have a wedding planner to frantically unbutton that bottom button, let's walk through suit types.

- **The Two-Button Suit:** The standard, classic suit is the two-button suit. The top button is generally buttoned while standing, and the bottom button is never buttoned. WHY IS IT THERE? Well. Life has to maintain a few mysteries.
- **The Three-Button Suit:** Are you tall? Do you have a very long torso? Okay. Then the three-button suit might work on you. The rules for the jacket can be remembered thusly: you sometimes button the top button, always button the middle button, and never button the bottom button.
- **The Double-Breasted Suit:** A double-breasted suit is a serious style statement, one that people love or love to hate. In this case, all suit buttons must remain buttoned while the jacket is on.
- **The Tux (Black Tie):** The classic tux has one button (button it). The differences between an expensive black suit and a tux are found in small details, such as satin facing on lapels, satin stripes on the leg, and cloth-covered buttons. It's

worth noting that tuxedos do not come with belt loops, and hence are worn with suspenders. Additionally, they should be paired with (shiny) tux shoes, and French-cut shirts with cufflinks.

- **Tails and Morning Suits:** It's assumed that a wedding dress is going to be the fanciest dress in the room. But that doesn't apply to suiting, which is expected to match the formality of the assembled guests. Which means, sadly, there are not a lot of chances to wear tails or a morning suit these days, as it's pretty hard to ask all your guests to wear *their* tails or morning suits. However, if you are brave and dashing enough to pull this off, my (top) hat is off to you.

RENTAL TUXES AND AFFORDABLE SUITS

Not that long ago it was standard practice for members of a wedding party to rent tuxes for weddings. That resulted in a lot of ill-fitting formalwear with billowing pants. As it's become increasingly common for suits to be worn at weddings, the popularity of rentals has decreased somewhat. Why? Well, renting a suit tends to cost roughly the same amount as buying an affordable suit, and the latter is pretty clearly a better investment.

If you want your wedding party in suits, go black, because many people already own a black suit.

— *continues* —

For folks who don't, you can give them options of renting or buying, with comparative price points. (Also: if one of your attendants doesn't have a suit and otherwise can't afford one, a reasonably priced suit makes a generous and useful attendant gift.) Yes, the suits won't all be identical, and no, you won't really notice. If you want some level of cohesion, give everyone the same—or a similar—tie.

However, if you're planning to outfit everyone in tuxes, you'll probably need to look at rentals, unless your crowd leans exceptionally formal.

If you choose rentals, start by doing a little research. Along with the old-school rental shops that serve everyone from kids attending their prom to folks in weddings, several online tux and suit rental companies have popped up in recent years. These specialize in formalwear that is higher quality, with better fit and more streamlined service.

Buying a Suit That Fits

If you go to any store that specializes in suits, the suit jackets will come finished, but the pants will come long and unhemmed. The assumption is that all suits need to be altered. Suits are made to be form fitting, and are in many ways far less forgiving than women's formal dresses. Although a visit to any suit specialist (a good department store will do fine) should provide you with pro-

fessionals who know everything there is to know about the fit of suits, here is a quick cheat sheet:

Select a suit that
- Fits in the chest
- Has a cut that you like
- Has pants that fit in the thigh, and ideally in the rear
- Has an appropriate jacket length (On men's suits, if you cup your hands, your fingers should be able to wrap around the bottom of the jacket. On women's suits, the jacket length can vary.)

Expect your suit to be altered
- In the arms (The arms of the suit are often taken up.)
- In the hem of the pants (Suits come unhemmed so they can be made to fit you precisely. They will be hemmed to have a short, medium, or full break—the fold created where the fabric hits the shoe—depending on your taste and the suit's style. Bring the shoes you'll wear for the wedding to your fitting.)

Suits are designed to fit well, yet in wedding after wedding, you'll see people wearing ill-fitting suits with pants so long that they look like they're going to be tripped over. Why is that? Suit separates. Suits are often sold, none too cheaply, as separates by outlets that don't specialize in suits. The idea is that you just pick something that fits well enough without bothering with tailoring. But you don't save a ton of money buying suits this way, so skip it for your wedding. Go to a store or department that makes a living selling suits, and get initiated into the world of people who know good tailoring.

And remember, if you want to invest in a quality suit that you will wear for years, you can consider a custom suit. If you go to a local tailor, prices can be reasonable. And if you can afford to treat yourself, an upscale custom clothier will do stunning work.

Suit Colors and Fabrics

If suiting has a lot of complicated-seeming rules, the traditional guidelines around color are blessedly simple. Lighter colors belong in the daytime; darker colors belong in the evening. Lighter fabrics are for summer; heavier fabrics are for winter.

Although you can make a statement with color or pattern in a suit (seersucker, anyone?), a safer way to make a statement is with the much more affordable shirt and tie.

MORE CASUAL GROOM STYLE

Because not every groom wants to wear a suit to get hitched, I asked APW's Maddie Eisenhart for her best style pointers for every level of wedding formality.

> Not every wedding is going to be suit-and-tie appropriate. But dressing more casually doesn't mean the general rules for formal wear aren't still a good idea. If you're going to wear jeans, for example, you still want to make sure they are tailored to fit well.

> If you have a beard before the wedding and are going to have a beard after the wedding, you do not have to shave your beard for the wedding. A good trim never goes amiss, but keep in mind that you want to look like the polished version of your everyday self, not the fancy version of someone else.

> Avoid getting a haircut the day or two before the big event. You want to leave some margin for error, and you need to give your hair a few days to settle into its new style.

> Boutonnières are 100 percent optional. (Yes, you can quote this to your mother-in-law.) If you want to wear one, don't try and hide the pin somewhere on the outside of your lapel. The pin goes on the back side of your lapel. If you're worried about getting stabbed, put a rubber earring back on the end for protection. For more on boutonnières, see Chapter 9.

> If you're getting married somewhere remote (read: with no cell service) and you don't know how to tie a tie, download a video directly to your phone, print out instructions, or otherwise have a friend or two nearby who can do it in their sleep.

ANDROGYNOUS STYLING OPTIONS, SUITS FOR WOMEN, AND OTHER GENDER-QUEER FASHION CHOICES

If you know you don't want to wear a dress but also don't want to be confined to a full-suit getup, well, the world is your oyster. Luckily, there are more and more resources for outside-the-gender-binary wedding and formalwear style choices online. Search for queer weddings, as well as queer styling resources, and get a sense of what other people have done. Do you want to wear a women's tux with pink accents and heels? Cowboy boots and a button-down? A suit and sweater vest with your hair in a faux hawk? A vest and bow tie with jeans? The options are nearly endless, and the inspiration out there is good and getting better every day. Fit your sense of personal style with the vibe you and your partner are aiming for with this wedding, and get styling.

However, for women or gender-queer folks who want to wear suits or some other kind of masculine-of-center dress for their weddings, fit can be a significant issue. Anita Dolce Vita from dapperQ.com says, "Many traditional mainstream brands still design suits according to the gender binary, offering either 'men's suits' or 'women's suits.' The cuts of these suits can be drastically different. For example 'men's' suit jackets generally button left-over-right, whereas 'women's' suit jackets generally button right-over-left." Suits made for men's bodies don't always transition seamlessly to non-male bodies, and solving those fit issues can take various amounts of energy and money. Here are some of the basic approaches you can take:

- **Get a custom suit from a progressive clothier.** There are (blessedly) an increasing number of brands focusing on suiting that's outside the gender binary. (Current standouts include companies like St. Harridan, Kipper Clothiers, Sharpe Suiting, Bindle & Keep, Jag & Co., Butch Clothing Company, Tomboy Tailors, and The Artful Gentleman.) Getting an outfit from one of these clothiers is an investment that will cost you as much as any wedding dress. However, unlike a wedding dress, you'll have plenty of opportunities to wear your suit again, and damn, will it look impeccable.

- **Get a men's suit (new or used) and have it tailored to fit.** This option can be more affordable, though it does have its issues. Because suits are cut to fit men's bodies, issues like shoulder pads (keep them in and possibly look like a linebacker? take them out and discover that the cut of the shoulder is now off?) often have to be dealt with. Try to find a tailor you trust to help you sort out what will work best.

- **Get a women's suit (and accessorize your way).** Women's suits are cut for bodies with curves, so they will often fit with significantly fewer modifications. That said, you have to decide if the styling works for you. One good thing about women's suits is that they come in a greater variety of cuts. Suits designed for men have jackets designed to cover the buttocks, whereas suits cut for women have jackets in a whole variety of lengths. You can also generally find women's suits in a wider variety of price points (including way more affordable options designed for occasional office wear).

No matter what you pick, feel free to accessorize with panache, and make the outfit yours.

Sparkles and Spreadsheets:
A Realist's Guide to Wedding Decor

8

THANKS TO THE INTERNET, AND EVery wedding magazine ever printed, it's easy to think that how your wedding looks is critical to the whole event, and hence the first thing you should plan. It's not. It's not the most important thing emotionally (duh), but it's also not the most important thing logistically.

DON'T PLAN YOUR WEDDING BACKWARD

If you start planning your wedding from your Pinterest board, it's not only going to be prohibitively expensive (those napkins individually hand edged in hot pink may cost a fortune), it also may not have much to do with the party you're actually throwing (you can't hang a disco ball at the beach).

So after taking a step back from Pinterest, and a moment to clear your head, think of how you plan any other party in your life. First, you start out with an idea of whom you're going to invite. What are their ages, tastes, and personalities? Then you move on to when and where you're going to have it. Your house? A nice restaurant? Once you've answered who, when, and where, you move on to what. What are you going to do to have fun? Drink cocktails? Dance? Have a three-legged race? What food and beverages are going to fuel that kind of fun? Then, and only then, do you think about how the party is going to look. And in reality, you might not even bother with much in the way of decor at all.

In real life, decorations are the layer of frosting we put on top of the already-made cake. We figure out what makes sense for the party we're throwing, and then we add balloons. In wedding land, people tend to treat decorations as the foundation of the event. But "glittery rustic" is a shaky thing to build a whole party on. So while you may have a Pinterest board (or four) for pretty weddings you'd like to throw, slow your roll for a moment. Make sure you've started with who's going to be there (Chapter 2) and where the party is going to be held and what time of day and what season it's going to happen in (Chapter 3). When you've got those issues solved, come back to decorations with a fresh eye. You may have been planning a beautiful industrial cocktail party with plenty of metallic accents. But if you just booked a daytime wedding in a garden, it's time to rethink things. As Alison Faulkner, the party planner behind The Alison Show, advises, "It's easier to work with your surroundings than to work against them." And when it comes to weddings, easy is best.

GET OFF THE INTERNET AND INTO YOUR VENUE

Decorations live firmly in the world of logistical reality, no matter how pretty they are. What can you afford? What can you transport? What will look good in your space? That's why when you start planning, it's good to get off of the Internet and into your venue, if at all possible.

•→· PRO TIP ·←•

Michelle Edgemont, Brooklyn wedding designer, suggests that if you're using a traditional wedding venue, you should spend a bit of time doing image searches for it online, as it's usually pretty easy to find pictures of weddings thrown in a particular event space. Look at the kinds of decorations people used previously. Figure out what you like, but also look at the scale of the decorations. Did a huge number of hanging pom-poms really bring the space alive? Did the centerpieces used look too large or too small? This will give you a place to start. If you're getting married in a private location, looking at pictures of similar weddings ("backyard weddings" "weddings in vacation rentals") can help you out.

To further root yourself in reality, start with your venue's list of decoration restrictions. (Chances are, they have some.) Common restrictions include open flames, attaching things to the wall, and moving the tables. Ruling those items out will narrow down your options.

Next, think about the time of day and the time of year of your wedding. A million tea lights is a kick-ass decor idea (if you're allowed open flames), but it's going to be near pointless if your wedding meal is at noon in a light-flooded room.

CREATING A DECOR PLAN

Once you've reoriented yourself from Pinterest to reality, it's time to start on a plan for your decor (and, ironically, probably to start a new Pinterest board). If, after pondering the reality of the situation, you've decided that your plan is about as complex as "put up some balloons and stuff," you can probably skip this section and call it a day. But, if you're wanting help logic-ing through a somewhat cohesive decoration scheme, here is a step-by-step.

THE RELAXED COLOR PALETTE

First up, you and your partner need to make some very basic decisions: What general colors are you going for? What is the general visual style and vibe that you want? Michelle Edgemont suggests that instead of picking the traditional two wedding colors, that you pick five to six colors, to create more of a palette. This can make decorating feel less restrictive and more organic. If you're organized, one or two of these colors can serve as your main color, and one or two can serve as your accent colors. If you're less, uh, focused, having a color palette can simply be a far more relaxing way to decorate.

GLITTER FABULOUS IS TOTALLY A STYLE

Once you've decided on a color palette, (let's not act like that's easy—we invested at least a month in fighting over ours) Alison Faulkner, the party planner behind The Alison Show, suggests selecting a basic visual style. Alison describes that process for an event she recently threw this way, "I chose a word 'Awesome' and a mood. From there I chose a style, loosely tropical and positive. How is positive a style? Well, I interpreted it as bright, poppy, bold." Although your wedding in no way needs

a theme, isolating a visual style or even a mood you want to convey can help you tie your design ideas together.

You might decide your visual style is, "things I like," or "stuff I can afford," or "objects that look reasonably good together." Embrace that. But for some people, picking a cohesive style is a way to make decorating decisions easier or give them better ideas. "Cute things" is vague, but "glitter industrial chic" can give you a little bit more guidance. Maybe you're going art deco, or rustic, or disco fabulous. Whatever it is, that unifying idea exists mostly to help simplify your choices.

YOU CAN'T DO ALL THE PROJECTS (SO PICK A FEW THAT MATTER)

Alright! So you've looked at your venue with a sensible eye and thought about what you could make work in the space. Then you and your partner picked a color palette and a general visual style. Maybe you even started a Pinterest board to go with it. Excellent.

Next up, your job is to isolate some projects that you think you might realistically be able to pull off. When you look carefully at professionally styled weddings on the Internet, you will realize that there is a cacophony of design projects taking over every square inch of the wedding. And that's fine, because those couples paid someone else to take care of the pretty. But assuming you have not hired someone else to decorate for you, you cannot take on even a fraction of the projects featured in these weddings. Which is fine. Because while no one ever objected to a cute coaster, that's not why your guests showed up to this party.

When selecting wedding projects, it's best to think of two metrics: the time it takes to produce them, and their visual and emotional impact at the event. You want the first metric to be as low as possible, and the second to be as high as possible. Plus, keep in mind that the best kind of wedding decoration is stylish buying, and that is in no way cheating. A bunch of paper pom-poms that you just have to hang up? Perfection.

DIY AND DECOR MANAGEMENT

Even if you're just shaking down your local party supply store for their best stuff, it's always important to plan for your DIY decor. Because even pom-poms need to be transported and set up. Here is what you should be thinking about.

Time management: Once you have an idea of what projects you're tackling, it's best to set up a general timeline of what you're doing when. Try to come up with realistic time estimates for each project. Is this going to take you a weekend? Thirty nights in front of the TV? One tipsy afternoon with five girlfriends? Michelle Edgemont notes that in the world of wedding crafting, "It's never one thing you have to make; it's always multiple." So before you take on making a hundred of something, make one and time yourself. Then do the math, allowing for oh-my-God-my-hands-hurt-I-can't-look-at-this-another-second breaks. And always start sooner than you think you need to.

Have a storage plan: Before you end up with a tiny apartment overflowing with oversized

continues —

crafts (and beer you need to haul to the wedding) come up with a storage plan. Which crafts are going to take up a lot of space? Which ones are going to shed glitter everywhere? If storing everything in your house isn't realistic, where else can you stash it?

Pack carefully: You want as many items as possible prepped before you pack them to go to the venue. In an ideal world, you won't be trying to finish a craft, or even trim candlewicks, once you get there. You'll just be pulling things out of boxes and setting them up. (For more detailed thoughts on packing for your venue, see pages 178–180.)

Installation: Your wedding is not going to set up itself. Make sure you allow time (and person power) for decorating the space. In most cases, you'll need to enlist family and friends to help you set up (unless you've hired a day-of coordinator) and assign different tasks to different people. If you have a bigger project that you need installed (say, a backdrop) or just more work than people, consider hiring a handyperson through a service like Task Rabbit (or another online forum) to do the heaving lifting and ladder climbing for you.

THE BIG UGLY SPACE PROBLEM

If, like one of the many people in recent history, you are getting married in the social hall of your religious institution, or a local community center, or your local veterans'

·•· PRO TIP ·•·

Alison Faulkner likes to make things do double duty. She says, "This is my major money-saving tip. What can you double-up on? Can you make the drink a decor item? Or can you make your decor a favor? Can you make your food decoration or your wall backdrop also a photo op?" This isn't to say you have to have any or all of these elements. But if you know you're going to pay good money for something (say, a name card), can you make it do something else as well? In an ideal world, can you make it play into the fun of the day (say, a favor that's also a photo booth prop)?

hall, you are probably facing some variant of the "big ugly space" problem. If you're planning a wedding in one of these big rooms, the decoration inspiration regularly dished out on the Internet can feel like it does not help you in any way.

Social halls come with their own, very specific set of decorating policies. There tend to be no "architectural elements" or "natural beauty" to highlight. Additionally, social halls are normally big. They often have terrifically high ceilings and are big enough to fit whole communities. This often means you have a scale problem with your decorations from the get-go. A small centerpiece is going to feel even tinier in a big space. You may not be filling up the space with your guests, and the chairs and tables that come with your venue (free, usually!) are not exactly the stuff of designer dreams.

That is what it is. If you are getting married in a community hall, your wedding isn't going to look like the weddings you see in trendy urban lofts, or sunny gardens, or even raw industrial spaces. It's going to look like a wedding in a hall, and luckily there is tradition and joy in that. So don't even bother trying to work against your space. You're not going to turn it into an Italian mansion, no matter how hard you try. Your goal is just to try to make it look festive. The one clear advantage is that these halls are generally pretty blank slates, so you can go a lot of places with decorations.

You'll want to decide early on what you can live with and what you can't. If your venue has bright-orange padded chairs, can you make that work, or do you want to splurge on chair covers? It's okay to decide to pay for an upgrade here or there (or everywhere, or nowhere), if that's going to work for you.

Otherwise, a lot of the guidelines of wedding design can still help you out. Pick some colors, pick a visual style . . . and then think about scale. If you want to make a big huge social hall look festive, you're going to

need a lot more of whatever you're decorating with than you think. So focus on decor items (see page 135) that you can afford to buy in bulk. If you're doing your own flowers, try to stick with lower-cost flowers that you can afford lots of (think of doing cool things with mounds of carnations). And if

·✦· PRO TIP ·✦·

Walking into a reception where you don't know everyone is a little overwhelming, and putting everyone at ease can go a long way toward creating a relaxed and fun celebration. Alison Faulkner points out, "When you show up to a party, you're feeling all vulnerable and confused. Do you know anyone? What should you do now that you're here? It doesn't have to be complicated. The answer can be: eat. The answer can be: sign a guest book. It can be: have a cocktail or make yourself a specialty soda. It doesn't need to be some huge organized thing or a game, but giving people a little bit of direction when they walk in the door helps them feel at ease, welcome, and ready to boogie." Remember that wedding guests also often want to know where they're sitting, so read up on seating charts and escort card boards on pages 171–174.

at all possible, order some test items, get into the venue with someone in your life who is good at spatial relationships, and have that person tell you about how many you need. Because one string of whatever it is probably isn't cutting it. And chances are, ten strings isn't, either.

Michelle Edgemont, who married in a social hall and designs weddings for a living, suggests using tall centerpieces (which don't have to be expensive, you just want them big), or Christmas lights hung low to visually lower the ceiling. Tori Hendrix says that color can go a long way. She likes to use cheap materials like muslin and paper in creative ways to pack a punch. Balloons are also great for filling a big space. And even though it might leave more empty space on the edges, push your tables together and make your dance space smaller. It makes the room feel cozy instead of cavernous.

ADVICE FOR MORE DECOR SITUATIONS

OUTDOOR SPACES

The good news about outdoor spaces is that they're pretty on their own. If you're getting married outside, feel free to put some chairs down (at least for the older or less healthy folks) and then just get married already.

But if you are going to do some decorations for an outdoor ceremony, focus on ways to frame your space. You might want

> **⤛ PRO TIP ⤜**
>
> Always plan for the worst. In many areas, this means having a rain plan (but you knew that). But remember to also plan for wind, which can whip away or knock over all your carefully crafted decorations in a second.

to put a table at the back of the seating, to hold programs or other decor. Creating some sort of backdrop for the vows can be nice, such as a wedding arch or chuppah. You can use two arrangements of flowers on either side of you for the same purpose. For a reception, use tricks to make the space seem more intimate, like drawing the eye down to the plate or table with decor items, and using candles or lights.

LOW-LIGHT SPACES

If your venue has particularly low light (or no light; for example, outside at night) evaluate if you'll need to provide additional lighting for basic safety and functionality (if not for mood). If you're aware that light may be an issue, try to see your venue under conditions similar to your wedding and assess what's needed. If you're working with a venue that has a staff, talk to them first. They've solved lighting problems many times and can give you advice on what works and what doesn't. Ask about lighting rentals or candles. (For more on lighting rentals, see page 41.) Consider using light-colored decor and linens to brighten up the space. And finally, remember to warn your photographer that light conditions will not be ideal, so that can be planned for.

VENUES WHERE YOU CAN'T ATTACH THINGS TO THE WALLS

It's common for venues to have limitations on what you can affix to walls. Imagine the same walls, used weekend after weekend, year after year, and you'll see why they might not want you sticking, and pounding, and taping the poor things. If your venue has these limitations, you'll need to find work-arounds for any decor you use. Balloons and tall centerpieces are always a great choice. In addition, you can search online for how to make a simple PVC backdrop frame (or buy a seamless backdrop frame used in photography). A frame will let you hang a backdrop or two without even touching the walls.

AFFORDABLE DECOR MATERIALS

Wedding designers are pros at turning nothing much into something awesome, so I polled some of my favorite design pros to ask what their suggestions are for affordable materials. Some of these items will surprise you (and make you run and look them up); some of them will simply remind you not to forget old standbys.

> Lots of candles
> Lighting: rented or smart use of the venue's lighting
> Anything paper: paper pom-poms, crepe paper, paper wedding bells, paper lanterns. Raid your local party supply store for ideas.
> Paper and glue (glitter paper, butcher paper, tissue paper, wrapping paper), just add creativity
> Rolls of seamless paper from photography stores
> Muslin
> Balloons
> Colored napkins
> Flagging tape (which is basically plastic caution tape, but in a variety of colors and patterns) used instead of ribbon
> Painter's drop sheets for backdrops
> Metallic spray paint, to make anything look appropriately festive
> Fruit
> Plastic animals, figurines, or other small affordable items, spray painted
> Vinyl, cut up and adhered to things creatively

Picking Flowers: Florists, DIY, and When the Bloom Is Off the Ranunculus

9

APW BASICS

1. Flowers are really pretty and have been around since more or less the beginning of weddings...

2. ...But you really, really, do not have to have flowers to make your wedding awesome.

3. DIYing flowers is a bigger undertaking than you might think. Mostly because unlike other craft materials, flowers die. So think twice before you take it on, and plan wisely.

4. It's not all or nothing. You can hire a florist to do your bouquets and DIY (or skip) centerpieces.

5. If you're hiring a florist, try to hire someone who's a good fit for your aesthetic... and trust that person.

FLOWERS GOT TIED TO WEDDINGS somewhere back in time immemorial (at a time when having flowers at your wedding meant picking some flowers). Now having blooms at a wedding means managing florists, flower markets, and floral foam. But for many of us, flowers are an integral part of the wedding tradition, and we're going to have them, by hook or by . . . floral shears.

The truth is, plenty of killer weddings have no flowers at all. You don't need centerpieces, but if you want them, non-floral centerpieces are a great make-in-advance option. You can hold something other than flowers walking down the aisle (a candle, a prayer book, a handkerchief), or hold nothing. So if you've been looking for an excuse to avoid flowers, take this one and run (away from the rest of this chapter).

For everyone else, this section will help you figure out if you want to hire a florist or go DIY (or a combo of both). The aim is to give you all the information you need to make your wedding flowers (almost) as easy as picking them in a field.

WHEN TO USE A FLORIST

If using a florist (or doing a combo of using a professional florist and adding a little DIY for backup) is a realistic financial possibility for you, I recommend it. There are lots of areas of wedding planning where DIYing is only slightly harder and vastly cheaper than hiring a pro. DIYing flowers is not one of those places. It's eminently doable, but given the fact that flowers have a limited life span, your prep has to happen right before the wedding. Plus, you'll need a reasonable amount of supplies and a bit of practice. This means the whole project can be more complicated and not as cheap as you might expect. In short, if you can afford to outsource all or part of your flowers, I advise that you do it.

FINDING A PROFESSIONAL FLORIST

If you're aiming to work with a professional florist, your first job is to figure out general price ranges in your area. Lots of florists won't list prices on their websites because floral prices are so dependent on the flowers used and the scope of the work. But some florists will give price ranges and starting prices, and that will start to give you the lay of the land. Warning: it may also give you sticker shock. (If it does, onward to the DIY flower section!)

Keep in mind that there are several kinds of professionals you can hire to do wedding flowers. Everyday florists produce work that usually isn't staggeringly creative, but it can be pretty affordable. Floral designers generally specialize in events and weddings. They tend to do beautiful, creative work and collaborate with their clients closely to create a specific vision, which comes with a higher price point. And full-service wedding designers will handle absolutely everything, from decorations to blooms, to chairs, and more.

Once you've figured out what you can generally afford, you can start making inquiries to get more specific quotes. Try to look for someone whose style matches your aesthetic. Because floral work is custom, you might not see something that exactly matches your vision in a florist's portfolio. But keep an eye out for basic styles. If you're spending a reasonable amount on flowers, you want to find someone who does what you love, instead of asking someone to play against his or her strengths.

·➤· PRO TIP ·➤·

Keep in mind that if you're looking to have a florist do one part of your wedding flowers but not all of them, you might need to do some calling around. Some florists will only take on full weddings; some will be happy to help you with smaller projects.

Working with a Florist

When you set up a consultation with a floral designer, it's good to go in with a little bit of your homework done. You should be straightforward about your budget. It will help the florist make smart suggestions and save everyone time. If you're going to be ordering centerpieces, it's best if you know what your table sizes will be. Designing centerpieces for long tables is totally different from designing for big round ones. And if you have something of a vision of what you want, come in with photos (here is where a Pinterest board is really helpful) and colors.

That said, make sure that you go into the meeting with an open mind. The flowers you have your heart set on might cost a fortune or be out of season. The florist might have savvy ideas you never would have thought of. Remember, you're hiring this person for his or her skill and experience, so take advantage of that.

And finally, always, always ask about extra fees. It's not good for anyone if you fail to factor a delivery or setup fee into your budget.

WHERE TO BUY WEDDING FLOWERS

A Wholesale Flower Market: If you live in or near an urban area and are looking for a large quantity of flowers, consider shopping at your local flower market. Most flower markets have hours for the general public and are a great source for a large variety of affordable in-season flowers.

Online Flower Wholesalers: There are increasing numbers of reputable online flower sellers who will ship fresh flowers directly to you. Talk to their customer service departments to figure out when the flowers should be delivered and if the blooms will need time to open. Also, order a little more than you think you need, just to cover your bases.

Your Local Grocery Store: If you're just looking to make bouquets, you can absolutely visit your local grocery store, gourmet food store, or big-box store the day before the wedding and buy whatever they have on hand for your bouquets. It's a quick, and affordable, solution.

FLOWER CHART

You don't need to know every flower in the encyclopedia to plan your wedding. (And let's be real, if you're paying someone else to do the flowers, you don't need to know a single one.) But sometimes it helps to be able to reference the basic facts: what's expensive and what's cheap, what's hearty and what's going to die if you look at it wrong. And, of course, if you have fallen head over heels in love with the peony (thanks, Internet), what flowers would provide a reliable substitute and cost less

FLOWER	SEASON	PRICE
Alstroemeria (Peruvian Lily, Lily of the Incas)	All year	$
Amaranthus	Aug, Sep, Oct, Nov, Dec, All year	$$
Anemone	Feb, Mar, Apr, May, Jun, All year	$$
Calla Lily	All year	$$$
Carnation	All year	$
Centaurea (Cornflower)	May, Jun, Jul, Aug	$
Cosmos (Chocolate Cosmos)	Mar, Apr, May, Jun, Jul, Aug, Sep	$
Craspedia (Billy Balls, Billy Buttons)	All year	$
Daffodil	Feb, Mar, Apr	$
Dahlia	Jun, Jul, Aug, Sep, Oct	$$$
Daisy (Cremon Mums, Pom Mums)	All year	$
Daisy, Gerber	All year	$
Delphinium (Larkspur)	All year	$
Dianthus (Sweet William)	Mar, Apr, May, Jun, Jul, Aug, Sep, Oct, Nov	$
Freesia	Mar, Apr, All year	$$
Gladiolus	Apr, May, Jun, Jul, Aug, Sep, Oct, Nov, Dec	$$
Gardenia	May, Jun, Jul, All year	$$$$$
Godetia	May, Jun, Jul, All year	$
Hyacinth	Mar, Apr, May, All year	$
Hydrangea	All year	$$$$
Iris	Mar, Apr, All year	$$

than your wedding dress? The chart on the next few pages is not meant to overwhelm you with information but to give you a handy reference guide in those stressful moments at the flower market, or when you realize you can't afford your Pinterest flowers.

FLORAL HACKS

Flowers do not need to be all pro or all DIY (something I dearly wish I'd figured out before our wedding). There is plenty of middle ground. Here are some of the options that may not have occurred to you.

HARDINESS	COLORS	ALTERNATIVES
****	all except blue	
****	green, red, more	Veronica
**	all; white with black center most popular	Godetia, Poppy, Ranunculus
***	white, gold, purple, many	Alstroemeria, Tulip
*****	white, pink, red, purple, yellow, orange, many	
**	blue	Scabiosa, Dianthus
*	copper, brown, deep maroon	Scabiosa, Zinnia, Dianthus
*****	yellow, green, orange, red	
****	yellow, white	
**	all except blue	Zinnia, Mum, Daisy, Poppy
****	white, yellow, pink, red, orange	
****	white, pink, red, purple, yellow, orange, many	
***	blue, purple, white	Gladiolus, Stock, Snapdragon, Lilac
*****	red, white, pink, fluffy green ball variety	Carnation
****	white, pink, red, purple, yellow, orange, many	
****	white, pink, red, purple, yellow, orange, many	Snapdragon, Hyacinth, Stock, Delphinium
*	white	Stephanotis, Magnolia, Dahlia, Rose
***	pink, red, white	Dianthus, Alstroemeria
***	purple, blue, white	Lilac, Snapdragon, Stock
***	white, blue, pink, green, tint	
***	blue, purple, yellow, white	

continues

FLOWER	SEASON	PRICE	
Lilac	Mar, Apr, May	$$	
Lily	All year	$$$	
Lily of the Valley	Dec, Jan, All year	$$$$	
Lisianthus	All Year	$$	
Magnolia	Apr, May, Jun, All year	$$$$	
Marigold	All year	$	
Mum (Chrysanthemum)	All year	$$	
Narcissus (Paperwhite)	Dec, Jan, Feb, Mar, Apr	$$	
Orchid	All year	$$$$$	
Peony	Apr, May, Jun, All year	$$$$	
Poppy	Feb, Mar, Apr, May, Jun	$$$$	
Queen Anne's Lace	Mar, Apr, May, Jun, All year	$$	
Ranunculus	Feb, Mar, Apr, May, All year	$	
Rose, Garden	All year	$$	
Rose, Long Stem	All year	$$	
Rose, Spray	All year	$	
Scabiosa	Dec, Jan, Jun, Jul, Aug, All year	$	
Snapdragon	All year	$	
Stephanotis	All year	$$	
Stock (Gillyflower)	All year	$	
Succulents	All year	$$$	
Sunflower	Jun, Jul, Aug, Sep, Oct	$$	
Sweet Pea	Mar, Apr, May, Jun	$$	
Thistle	All year	$	
Tulip	Feb, Mar, Apr, May, All year	$$	
Veronica (Speedwell)	All year	$	
Zinnia	Jul, Aug, Sep, Oct	$$	

	HARDINESS	COLORS	ALTERNATIVES
	***	white, purple	Hyacinth, Snapdragon, Stock
	****	many	Godetia, Dianthus, Stock, Delphinium
	***	white	Queen Anne's Lace, Narcissus, Stephanotis
	**	white, purple, light green, pink	Godetia
	***	white, pink, purple	Dahlia, Lily, Peony
	*****	orange, gold, yellow, red	Mum, Carnation, Daisy
	*****	many	
	***	white, yellow	Stephanotis, Daffodil
	**	many	Iris
	**	white, pink, red, many	Ranunculus, Poppy, Garden Rose, Mum, Tulip
	*	red, orange, yellow, more	Ranunculus, Anemone
	****	white, green	
	****	all except blue	
	****	all except blue	
	****	all except blue	Lisianthus, Other rose varieties
	****	all except blue	
	**	maroon, burgundy, lavender, white	
	***	white, yellow, pink, lavender, many	
	***	white	Narcissus
	***	white, pink, red, purple, yellow, orange, many	Snapdragon, Hyacinth
	*****	green, gray, purple, black, pink	
	****	yellow, orange, gold, red, black	Zinnia, Mum
	*	white, red, pink, purple, many	
	*****	blue, green, gray, gold	
	***	all except blue	
	***	white, blue, purple, pink	
	****	all of them	Dahlia, Daisy, Mum

DIY Bouquets and No-Big-Deal Centerpieces

On the day of your wedding, chances are the flowers you end up caring about the most are the flowers that you're holding. There is nothing wrong with wanting that bouquet to be crafted with more skill than you've got (even after watching a bajillion YouTube tutorials). If you feel like the cost of a florist for your entire wedding is out of reach, consider enlisting a florist to do your bouquets only. That is likely to cost the same (or less) as it would cost you to DIY all your flowers on your own. You can then do simple DIY centerpieces, non-floral centerpieces, or just skip center-pieces altogether. (Note that if you're only ordering bouquets, your florist might not offer delivery.)

If you really want fresh flowers to hold as you walk down the aisle but only care about centerpieces insofar as they make the tables look pretty, consider DIYing your bouquet and creating non-floral cen-terpieces in advance . . . or just skip them.

Floral Consulting and DIY Flowers

Some florists (and wedding planners!) of-fer consulting with couples planning to DIY their wedding flowers. If you can find someone in your area who offers this ser-vice, jump on it. You'll save far more than the consulting fee with advice on what (and how much) to buy, and what to skip.

DIYING ALL OF YOUR WEDDING FLOWERS

When contemplating DIYing your wed-ding flowers, it's important to think about the scope of the endeavor. Putting to-gether a centerpiece isn't actually all that hard. But the whole picture looks more like this: figuring out your design, buying vases and floral supplies, practicing, buying your wedding flowers right before the wedding, keeping them alive, putting centerpieces together, and having enough space in a ve-hicle to transport them to the venue. All together it's a *project*. It's a totally doable project, but if you take it on, either mini-mize it (bouquets only), or make it one of your only major projects for the wedding.

To help make your DIY florals as success-ful as possible (fewer dead flowers, fewer tears), Natalie Marvin, owner of Belle Flower, and Jessica Dixon, owner of The Petal Company, shared their best tips and tricks for making your florals awesome and painless.

- **Come up with designs in advance.** Getting in the room with pretty flow-ers doesn't mean that inspiration will suddenly strike or that you'll have any clue how to construct a centerpiece or a bouquet. This is the time to scour the Internet for inspiration pictures of projects you think you could actually create, and ideally you should find tutorials for them. Also, hit up YouTube to watch videos on how to put together a bouquet. Get some flowers from the grocery store and practice.

- **Don't get too technical.** You know all those amazing, lush, complex centerpieces you've seen on Pinterest? I say this with great love, but you can't have those if you're DIYing. You want to pick a design with one or two flowers, and make sure you have a good idea of how to construct the thing.

- **Buy your vases.** Buying vases can work one of two ways: you can figure out what your concept is and find vases to match, or you can find vases that seem workable and figure out what flowers to put in them. Regardless, be aware of scale. Something that seems huge to you at home may well be dwarfed by a large round table. Great sources for vases are flower markets, craft stores, thrift stores, big-box stores, and Amazon. You can always do some crafting to make your vases cooler (hello, spray paint), but you really don't have to.

- **Buy floral supplies.** You'll want to pre-buy your supplies, which you can easily do online. You'll probably want floral scissors, floral tape, pins (for your bouquets as well as any corsages), flo-

ral foam (as needed), and floral wire (if you're doing boutonnières and corsages). Don't forget ribbon to wrap the bouquets.

- **Pick hardy flowers.** When doing it yourself, you don't want to risk your money on flowers that die if not treated exactly right or that only last twenty-four hours. Research which flowers will last longer (see pages 140–143 for our flower list) and use those blooms. When you get the flowers, put them directly into clean water and remove leaves and foliage below the water line. Store them in a cool, shady place.

- **Be aware of how the flowers may arrive.** If you're ordering from a wholesale flower company, make sure you know what state the flowers will arrive in. Often they will be delivered a few days early, still closed, and you need to keep them alive while they bloom. Allow time for that, and make sure someone is going to be in charge of keeping them fresh.

- **Arrange for help.** Unless you're only doing simple bouquets, you're going to need several sets of hands to put the flowers together. Arrange a time (probably the day before the wedding) to do the arranging. Remember to have pictures on hand of what the final product is supposed to look like and set up a sample or two to copy. Once all the flowers are done, you may want to do a little quality control to make sure they look the way they're supposed to.

- **Timeline (it always takes twice as long as you think).** Centerpieces can be created two days out. Plan for two to three hours for fifteen centerpieces, with two people working. Bouquets should be made the day before. Allowing for inexperience, allot forty-five minutes to an hour for a bridal bouquet, and about half that time for each attendant bouquet. Boutonnières and corsages are tricky little things and have to be made the day before or the day-of to stay alive. Allow two hours for a handful of them. (But even better advice is to skip them, as they are hard to do as an amateur.)

- **Don't refrigerate your flowers.** I know, what? But as it turns out, the humidity and temperature of a normal refrigerator is different from that of a floral fridge, and it will dry out your flowers and kill them. Store your flowers in a cool and shady place, and you'll be fine.

- **Arrange for transportation.** Unless you're one of those lucky people with nearly unlimited access to your venue (maybe it's your house?), chances are good that you're going to have to prep your flowers in a different location and transport them to the venue. Transporting centerpieces takes space (you can't stack them) and careful packing. One option is to use opaque vases and create your centerpieces in floral foam, so they'll stay in one piece even if they fall over. Another option is to empty the water from the vases, and pack things together compactly so nothing gets knocked around too badly. Regardless, plan in advance for a friend or loved one with truck or van space to transport the flowers.

Ceremonies, Vows, and
Why We're All Here

10

✤ APW BASICS ✤

1. Although the whole wedding industry focuses on things it can sell you, the real magic of the wedding is the ceremony. It's the part where you make huge promises to each other and actually get hitched.

2. Regardless of whether you're having a traditional religious wedding or you're making it all up from scratch, spend some time with the ceremony to make it feel like it's yours.

3. If you have an emotional and personal ceremony, it sets the tone for the day. (And it means no one will remember that you skipped centerpieces.)

4. You don't have to write your own vows if you don't want to. Traditional vows are time tested, meaningful, and phenomenally lovely.

5. In ten years, you probably won't care what color your bridesmaid dresses were. But you might well care what you promised each other. So take some time to carve that into your hearts.

◆

DURING THE PLANNING PROCESS, people often focus on things like dresses, decor, and flowers, but all of those things are actually pretty ancillary to the main event: the ceremony.

At its core, a wedding is the occasion when two people get hitched. The rest of it is just a party. Even though this is the honest-to-god factual truth, somehow the real *wedding*—the ceremony and the vows—gets swept aside. And then, somewhere in the vicinity of the last minute, there is a general feeling of panic that the wedding ceremony hasn't been written, or "OMG we're getting married tomorrow, what about our vows??" and everyone stays up far too late trying to throw something together. My hope is to save you from that—or at least give you some killer resources so that if you are pulling this whole thing together last-minute, you can do it with confidence.

This chapter provides resources for those of you who are writing your own ceremonies and vows, though it may also be useful for people modifying faith-based ceremonies. For those of you who will be having a traditional religious wedding of one sort or another, congratulations! You're pretty much done. One of the wonderful things about, say, a full Mass wedding is that you can remove "writing your ceremony and vows" from your to-do list. (However, if you're allowed to pick your own music and readings, move on to "Fit In the Fun Stuff" on pages 150–151.)

Regardless of whether you're writing your own ceremony, having a traditional ceremony that's meaningful for the two of you, or doing something in between, think of it this way: with a really emotional, personal, and lovely wedding ceremony, everyone will think your wedding is the best ever right from the start. They'll be so overwhelmed with emotion that they'll pretty much fail to notice if you skipped centerpieces and didn't serve their favorite food.

A good ceremony is basically the ultimate wedding hack.

PICK A THESIS

Mixing the words "thesis" and "wedding" sounds crazy, I know. But spending time figuring out what your ceremony means to the two of you is time well spent. Think of it like free premarital counseling that also simplifies and streamlines your ceremony-writing process.

·✦· PRO TIP ·✦·

Officiant Jenny Dreizen from Cheerleader For Love explains the idea behind creating a thesis this way: "A thesis makes the whole ceremony cohesive and much easier to create. For example, is your message, 'We took a journey together and this is the ultimate journey we start today,' or 'Our love has been tested and today we reaffirm our connection,' or 'Woohoo! FINALLY!'? Is your tone nostalgic? Forward thinking? Is your ceremony aimed toward the community of loved ones there to celebrate and witness your love, or is it more about the team of two you've created with your partner?"

Your thesis could be as simple as up-holding the time-honored traditions of marriage in your religion or culture, or it could be far more creative. The idea here is simply to focus on what your goals are for your ceremony, and to think and talk about what marriage means for the two of you.

Coming up with an idea to tie together your ceremony will help you craft and se-lect any additional elements you may want to include, from personal vows to readings to music to prayers. It gives you a way to figure out what fits within your wedding service, and what does not.

LEGAL REQUIREMENTS

Within the US, legal requirements vary so much between states (and change so fast) that there is no point trying to compre-hensively round them up here. Throw in other countries, and the sky is the limit. However, here is a list of common requirements and limitations surrounding legal marriage. Take this as a re-minder to do your research about your location of choice, and then jump through all the hoops.

> **Getting Your License (Time Frame and Possible Waiting Periods):** You can't just waltz off to your wedding and get legally married. You've got to get your license first (normally from your local city hall). Most localities have a window of time before the wedding during which you can get your li-cense. Some places also have a mandated waiting period between getting your li-cense and getting hitched.

> **Blood Tests:** Some states require them. The few states that do are generally testing for STDs (though not HIV) and genetic dis-eases such as sickle-cell anemia or Tay-Sachs disease.

> **Premarital Counseling and Education:** This is no longer required by states, but some encourage it by reducing the mar-riage license fee for those who participate in a state-sponsored course. Most states just give you a delightfully out-of-date edu-cational pamphlet.

> **Wedding Location:** Fun fact: in England you cannot get legally married outside. In the US, there are not normally such strict location requirements, but if you're getting married abroad, make sure to check on lo-cal laws (and local work-arounds).

> **Solemnizing the Wedding:** Different lo-calities have different rules about who can make it legal. Some states only allow the usual suspects: judges, clergy, and county clerks. Some states allow family and friends to be ordained online or deputized by the county to perform the ceremony, but some do not. (If you're set on having a friend perform the ceremony, remember that you can always do the legal bit at city hall.) In Colorado and D.C., couples can self-solemnize their own marriages.

— *continues* —

> **Sober and of Right Mind:** Not to spoil your fun, but you do have to be sober and legally sane during the signing of a marriage license.

> **Declaration of Consent:** It is common that there must be a verbal declaration of consent for a legal marriage to take place. If that's required where you are, make sure to include that in your service, if you are writing your own.

> **Witnesses:** Most states require one to two witnesses to both see the ceremony performed and sign the documents. This doesn't spoil your super-secret elopement plans, though. Officiants and courthouse workers are usually honored to witness your wedding, as are photographers (if you have one). If you're having a more traditional wedding, remember that being a witness is an honor you can give out.

> **Consummation:** Some states still require this. You're welcome?

PUTTING THE WORDS TOGETHER

Sitting down with a blank piece of paper and an idea that you're going to write your wedding service—from scratch—can be more than a little daunting. But the good news is that this is one of those areas where there is no point in totally reinventing the wheel. The world is filled with such a beautiful variety of wedding services, you can easily find a place to start. (Plus, a good

wedding service is all *about* plagiarism.) In fact, no matter how traditional or outside of the box your ceremony is, the way to approach the basic construction of a meaningful wedding ceremony is the same.

PICK A STRUCTURE

First up, pick a structure for your service. This might be as simple as saying, "We're having the Hindu kind!" or it might mean perusing the list on pages 153–154 of wedding ceremonies the world over, picking a few things that speak to you, and coming up with a format never used before. It doesn't matter which route you take, your job right now is just to pick a basic framework to guide you. Take a look at "The Building Blocks of a Wedding Service" and start assembling your basic structure.

FIT IN THE FUN STUFF

After you've picked your structure (and maybe even settled on a thesis, as covered on pages 148–149), it's time to figure out what flexibility you have within that structure, and how you want to use it. This is the point where you get to add music and readings (you know, the good stuff), and otherwise flesh out your service—religious or otherwise—with nuance and personality.

If you're having a traditional service, start by talking to your clergy member to find out exactly what can be added and subtracted from your service. Almost all traditional services have room for you to get a little creative with things like readings, music, and prayers. When the bulk of your service is set, it's important to really think about the choices you do have. Even if you're picking text from within a holy book or a holy music tradition, there are usually a variety of writings and music that you can choose from, so don't limit yourself to the greatest hits.

If you're crafting a non-traditional service, you have the advantage and disadvantage of the sky being the limit. Being able to pick anything in the world can be a mite overwhelming. Stick to music and texts that are meaningful to you, and keep your thesis in mind as you plan. You don't have to craft the most original ceremony the world has ever seen, and it's fine if you choose a reading that is popular at weddings. As long as one or both of you find it meaningful, it's a good choice.

A CHECKLIST FOR OFFICIATING A CEREMONY

So your friends or loved ones asked you to officiate their wedding! Although you're probably honored, you may also not quite know where to start. This list aims to give any amateur officiant a little bit of guidance. (And to get rid of that nagging feeling that you're probably forgetting *something*.)

> Find out the legal requirements for ordination in the location where the wedding will take place. (Keep in mind that in the US, requirements can vary somewhat by state.) Will online ordination be sufficient? Do you need to register with the county clerk's office? Call and find out.

> Get ordained online if you need to. Registering online with the Universal Life Church takes about thirty seconds and is free. (Getting a certificate mailed to you costs a few dollars.)

> Get the marriage license from the couple well in advance, or triple-check that they will remember to bring it to the ceremony.

> Talk through the ceremony and vows with the couple. Have a conversation about what they want the vibe and the length of the service to be. As the master of ceremonies, you'll set the tone.

> Figure out if the couple wants you to make an address during the ceremony. If they do, talk about what approach feels right and what length they'd prefer. Then write it . . . ideally not the night before.

> Talk through the logistics of the service. Who are the main players, and where will they stand? Are there ritual elements needed? (Glasses to break, brooms to jump, candles to light, etc.) If so, how will they get to the ceremony, and where should they be placed?

> Figure out what you'll be reading from. Will it be a binder? A music stand? A podium? Ask about amplification. (For more see page 41.)

— *continues* —

> Print out a copy of the whole ceremony in large print, and bring it in some sort of folder. This should include any announcements you need to make before or after the ceremony, a full copy of the service, extra copies of the vows, and extra copies of the readings.
> Discuss your attire with the couple (and wear comfortable shoes).
> Figure out who is running the rehearsal, and what your role is. Make sure to check in with the wedding planner, day-of coordinator, wedding stage manager, or whoever is in charge of logistics.
> Speak slowly, clearly, and loudly.
> After the ceremony, have the couple sign the license.
> Remember to mail in the license within the legal time limit.

Congratulations! You just married a couple!

THE BUILDING BLOCKS OF A WEDDING SERVICE

Most Western wedding services are created with the same fundamental building blocks. Although you don't have to include all of these elements in your wedding service, it can be helpful to look at a list of what is included as you begin to construct your own ceremony. Be sure to confirm your state's legal requirements for declaration of intent and any other mandatory ceremony requirements. Use items on this list, mix and match with inspiration from

-•- PRO TIP -•-

APW contributor Elisabeth Snell has officiated for several friends' weddings, and she offers this perspective, "What I found critical (and difficult!) was my role as General Ceremony Tone-Setter. If you're the one standing up there, guests will be looking expectantly at you and taking your cues for what the overall mood is going to be. Even though your precise words or your outfit may not linger, how you say what you say, and how you manage the emotion and energy of the room will contribute to how everyone remembers the ceremony." So in addition to showing up with your binder of words, show up calm, emotionally present, and focused.

wedding services around the world (see pages 153–154), and come up with something that works for you.

- **Opening/Welcome:** This can include a welcome of your guests by your officiant, a blessing, a statement to set the tone for the service, or just a reminder to turn off cell phones (or not take photos, if that's your preference).
- **Expression of Intent:** The declaration of intent comes in many different forms

but is generally what we think of as "I do." In most places it is legally required that both members of the couple verbally consent to the wedding taking place, and this is where that happens.

- **Readings, Hymns, and Prayers:** These are incorporated into the service to give it color and emotional richness, but if you want to create a very short service, skip them. They are, however, a great way to honor people, and to honor your cultural history or your respective cultures. Keep in mind that though these readings traditionally come from religious texts, they can come from anything that inspires you.
- **Address or Sermon:** This is when your officiant speaks a bit about marriage, and often about your personal relationship. For clergy, the sermon might put your marriage into a religious context. Regardless of whether you're having a friend or a clergy member officiate, it's okay to ask what form the address or sermon usually takes and what you can expect.
- **Vows:** This is the portion of the service when you make promises to each other. They may be traditional, "For better or for worse," or something you write yourself. (More on vows on pages 155–162.)
- **Ring Ceremony:** The rings can be exchanged during the wedding vows, though they are often exchanged afterward with simple ring vows, "With this ring, I thee wed."

- **Pronouncement:** This is when the officiant introduces you to the crowd, in whatever form you prefer. "I give you the new wife and wife!" "I now present to you the Martin-Guzmans!"
- **The Kiss:** Hooray!

WEDDING CEREMONIES: MANY CULTURES, MANY WAYS

If you're writing your own secular service, it can often be hard to get beyond the basic Christian outlines of a ceremony because it's what we see over and over again in every movie and TV show. But weddings come in many forms in various cultures. Here are some very different ways that weddings take place in different religions. Cultural appropriation is never a great idea; rather, I'm hoping this helps you think outside the box, as you work to figure out what you want your wedding ceremony to look like.

> **Quaker Ceremony:** The ceremony, like other Quaker meetings, takes place in silence, with people rising to speak as they are so moved. The couple states their promises to each other, with the idea that they are married by God, and the marriage is witnessed by those in attendance. At the end of the service, those in attendance are asked to sign a marriage certificate in witness, which is then displayed in the couple's home.

— *continues* —

> **Eastern Orthodox Ceremony:** The Eastern Orthodox wedding ceremony takes place in two distinct parts. The first part of the service—consisting of the exchange of rings and often the declaration of consent—is equated to the civil service and takes place in the vestibule of the church closest to the secular world. From there, the couple makes their procession into the church, and in doing so brings their relationship into God's kingdom. There are no spoken vows, as the couple's presence is considered their consent. The couple is crowned as part of the service.

> **Jewish Ceremony:** The basic elements of the Jewish wedding include the signing of a *ketubah* (a legal marriage document), the ceremony and ring exchange under a chuppah (wedding canopy), and the seclusion of the couple after the ceremony, known as *yichud*. Common ritual elements include seven circles (originally of the bride around the groom, now often of the couple around each other), the singing of seven blessings, the drinking of wine, and the breaking of a glass. Notably, though a rabbi is present during the ceremony, the couple marries each other by reciting vows, with the rabbi serving as witness.

> **Muslim Ceremony:** Much like Jewish weddings, Muslim weddings have a few key parts. There is the exchange of the *mahr*, or the marriage gift, which can be in the form of cash or personal property, given from the groom to the bride. There is a declaration of consent and acceptance, followed by the signing of a legal document. A marriage sermon is given by a respected member of the community. Although some modern Muslim ceremonies do incorporate vows, it isn't a historically traditional part of the service.

> **Hindu Ceremony:** Although there is no standard Hindu ceremony, there is a set of basic rituals on which a service tends to be based. These rituals include the *baraat* (the arrival of the groom and groom's family), the *kanyadaan* (the giving away of the daughter), and the *sankalpa* (the couple garlanding each other to signal mutual approval to move forward). The ceremony itself physically takes place around a sacred fire. The most important component is the seven-step ritual, in which each step represents a vow that one partner makes to the other.

> **Buddhist Ceremony:** Marriage is not a sacred ceremony within Buddhism. Because of this, a wedding is expected to be a generally secular affair, which takes place according to the guidelines of the local government, usually with a blessing by a monk at a temple after the wedding, as the temple is seen as the center of the community. That said, many practitioners do include Buddhist thought and practice in their ceremonies, sometimes incorporating the five precepts into vows, along with rituals such as hand washing, offering gifts to Buddha, offerings to monks, and the lighting of candles and incense.

WEDDING VOWS: ENGRAVE THEM ON YOUR HEART

If the ceremony is, well, the actual wedding (not, you know, the reception), then the vows are the emotional core of the ceremony. Your vows, and whatever words you choose for them, are the reason everyone is together. The moment when you say them is the moment that you make huge promises to each other, and actually get married. The vows are the reason for the whole celebration.

Which isn't to say that you should commence freaking out about your vows and become totally paralyzed by the thought of coming up with them. Instead, think of this as an invitation to stop worrying about the seating chart for five seconds, and think about why you're actually throwing this damn party.

To Write or Not to Write

First, let's debunk the myth that you have to write your wedding vows for your wedding to be meaningful. You don't. There is power in saying the words that generations of people have said before you, or words that tie you to a particular faith tradition. Plus, over thousands of years, there has been a real perfection of the language of vows. I mean, "For better or for worse, for richer or for poorer, in sickness and in health. . . . " Good luck trying to beat that for economy of language and getting right to the heart of the issue.

For those of you who are not tied to the vows of a particular faith but who still want traditional-ish vows, see pages 159–160 for a compiled list of religious vows. It's a good reminder of the huge variety that exists within one small genre, and it can serve as inspiration to create your own. Take your pick, or mush a few together!

For those of you who want to write your vows from scratch, I've got plenty of advice and a list of non-traditional vows that other couples have used (pages 161–162). When it comes to wedding ceremonies, sometimes the best form of creation is artful stealing.

But mostly, don't overthink it. Writer Jen Girdish explains, "I went through almost every book in my library for inspiration. Then, one day we decided on a reading from a Ruth Krauss and Maurice Sendak children's book called *I'll Be You and You Be Me*. I realized that everything I love about children's books—the ability to communicate complicated emotions in simple sentences—was perfect. No need for perfect, overly articulate compound sentences." Say what you mean. Mean what you say. It's that simple.

Breaking Down Vows into Parts

What's often thought of as the wedding vows is actually a conglomeration of three elements of the service: declaration of consent, vows, and ring vows. When constructing a service or writing your own vows, this matters. One element tends to be legally required, and the others are not. So, using the most movie-traditional words, let's review the parts of what we all think of as wedding vows:

The Declaration of Consent:

OFFICIANT: Do you Alex, take Sam, to be your husband/wife? Will you love her/him, comfort her/ him, honor and keep her/him, in sickness and in health as long as you both shall live?

ALEX: I do.

The Vows:

I, Alex, take you, Sam, to be my lawfully wedded (husband/wife), to have and to hold, from this day forward, for better, for worse, for richer, for poorer, in sickness and in health, until death do us part. This is my solemn vow.

The Ring Vows/Ring Ceremony:

With this ring, I thee wed.

In most locations, a declaration of consent is legally required (and it also happens to be included in most wedding ceremonies around the world). It is often included very early in the ceremony, to set the tone, with the vows and ring ceremony coming near the end.

However, not all cultures include vows as part of the ceremony. Similarly, not all cultures exchange rings as part of the wedding ceremony (though most cultures do exchange some item of value).

HOW TO WRITE YOUR VOWS

Writing your own wedding vows has become such a common part of the wedding ritual, that it's easy to assume, "Obviously we'll be doing this!" without stopping to check and see if you both want to. Or hell, if you're even allowed to. So before you dive into writing, take a quick time-out. First up, do you both want to write them? And second, what's your goal for your vows? If you simply want your vows to sound like the traditional ones, pick something you like from pages 161–162 and go take a nap. But, if you both want to make sure your vows are personal reflections of your relationship and clearly reflect the promises you want to make to each other, read on.

Check with your officiant. If your wedding is being officiated by a friend, or someone you hired, let's assume vow writing is a go. But if your wedding is taking place within a religious institution, it's likely that you'll have the option, or even be required, to use certain vows. If you want to contribute something personal, ask what form you might use for that. Sometimes you can add a personal set of vows, after you say the time-honored vows. And other times you might be able to contribute something like a personal couple's prayer. Find out what forms of self-expression might be encouraged in your religious ceremony, and then see what works for you.

Research. If there is one piece of writing that might well give you crippling writer's block, it might be dashing off a few promises that, you know, encompass the rest of your life. Instead of starting from scratch, look through examples of other couples' work (see pages 161–162) and time-honored vows (pages 159–160) and pick out a few things that really strike a chord with you. Compare with your partner, and see where your common ground is.

Decide on a structure and a tone. The goal is to have your vows feel like two parts of a whole. They don't need to mirror each other exactly, but you do want them to feel like they belong at the same wedding. You don't want one vow that's heartfelt and one that's jokey. So pick a format. Is it "I promise . . . " or is it a list of things you love about the other person? What's the tone you're going for? Lighthearted and loving, or life-changing statements? Figure out what you want your vows to accomplish, and what form and tone will serve you best, and then get started. You might also want to discuss length. No one wants to read off a two-sentence vow and be greeted with a five-page essay in return. Setting a rough word count can help your vows mirror each other.

To surprise or not to surprise. Jen Girdish sums up the dilemma this way, "My husband and I like to surprise each other—we're also a little too competi-tive—so the surprise element was fun. It felt like wrapping a gift for him. How-ever, a friend of mine got upset because he didn't think his vows were as good as his wife's. It's a good idea to consider what kind of people you and your partner are and whether or not the element of sur-prise would actually be fun or another stress point." If you decide it's easier to write your vows together, hearing them out loud on your wedding day will still feel like the best kind of revelation.

Set aside time to write. Staying up late the night before your wedding to figure out your vows sounds romantic in theory, but it's stressful in practice. Instead, take some time to brainstorm and draft. And if you really want to go romantic, consider having a night away (or a night in with a nice bottle of wine) and make a love-you-forever evening of it.

Practice. When you look back at your wedding years from now, it's probably not going to matter to you very much what trendy-at-the-time color you picked for your best people. What you'll be thinking about (in your best and worst moments) is, "What exactly did I promise this person again?" So, you want to practice your vows to make sure you don't freeze and flub them on the day-of, but you also want to practice them to embed this most important bit of wedding-ness in your brain.

Remember they are yours. You mom might weigh in on the wedding happen-ing in a church. Your BFF might suggest bridesmaid dress colors. But the vows belong to only the two of you. Do what makes you happy. Do what will help you through the hard times. Make the promises you want to guide you through the many long years of your life, and do it in a way that feels right to you both.

INTERFAITH SERVICES: THE BASICS

Planning a wedding ceremony can be difficult, but planning an interfaith service adds its own challenges. An interfaith or a faith/no-faith service is hard, but it's hard for a reason. As you have conversations about what you want your wedding service to look like, you're also navigating the moral and ethical conversations that create the outline of your family's spiritual and cultural life. More than that, you may well be involving your wider family in these conversations for the first time. It's not fun to realize that your partner has an allergic reaction to the idea of Jesus being mentioned in his or her wedding ceremony, and that your mother can't stop crying over the idea of Jesus not being mentioned. But it is important information. The same questions and compromises are going to come up over and over again—at holidays, on religious occasions, and if you have kids. None of it is easy. But it is useful. Better to have these conversations now, rather than screaming over a newborn you can't

decide whether to baptize or circumcise (or both).

Emotions aside, planning an interfaith service can be complex when it comes to deciding on both clergy and location. Many clergy members across many faiths have policies that prevent them from officiating interfaith services, and those that will officiate often have limitations around the kinds of services that they will officiate. For example, it's not uncommon that Jewish clergy will not officiate services where Jesus is mentioned (talk about tricky). Many clergy members will also not officiate services that take place in a house of worship outside their own faith—meaning that many interfaith services take place outdoors, or in neutral settings (which isn't a bad idea anyway). It can be hard not to take these limitations personally, particularly if they conflict with your goals for your service. But as the Reverend Dr. Nicholas C. Ciccone Jr., says in his introduction to *Celebrating Interfaith Marriages*, "It is important to understand that interfaith marriages are impacting every religious community in this country, and each community is struggling to find ways to meet this challenge while maintaining their beliefs and customs."

As someone who struggled through her own interfaith wedding planning, my best advice is to ask lots of questions. If a clergy member says no, ask why. (Chances are there is a well-thought-through reason, even if it's one you don't agree with.)

If this person can't meet your needs, ask for advice on other officiants who might be able to work with you. If your partner has a strong opinion on something, ask questions to understand why (you're going to be living with this reasoning for a lot of years). And with family, mix "why" questions with clear delineations of boundaries. At the end of the day, the two of you have to come up with your own rules for your interfaith wedding and household. No matter how strong your dad's feelings on a particular subject are, this is your decision to make.

RELIGIOUS WEDDING VOWS

Here is a selection of wedding vows from religions in which they are traditionally a part of the wedding service.

Episcopal

In the Name of God, I, Sam, take you, Alex, to be my [wife/husband],
to have and to hold from this day forward, for better for
worse, for richer for poorer, in sickness and in health, to love
and to cherish, until we are parted by death. This is my
solemn vow.

Hindu

With the first step, we will provide for and support each other.
With the second step, we will develop mental, physical, and spiritual strength.
With the third step, we will share the worldly possessions.
With the fourth step, we will acquire knowledge, happiness, and peace.
With the fifth step, we will raise strong and virtuous children.
With the sixth step, we will enjoy the fruits of all seasons.
With the seventh step, we will always remain friends and cherish each other.

continues —

Roman Catholic

I, Sam, take you, Alex, to be my [wife/husband],
I promise to be true to you in good times and in bad,
in sickness and in health.
I will love you and honor you all the days of my life.
Alex, take this ring as a sign of my love and fidelity
in the name of the Father, and of the Son, and of the Holy Spirit.

Unitarian

I, Sam, take you, Alex, to be the [wife/husband] of my days,
to be the parent of my children, to be the companion of my house.
We will keep together what measure of trouble and sorrow our lives may lay upon us,
and we will share together our store of goodness and plenty and love.

Jewish

Harei at m'kudeshet li b'taba'at zo kedat Moshe v'Yisrael.
Behold, you are consecrated to me with this ring according to the laws of Moses and Israel.
V'erastikh li l'olam, v'erastikh li b'tzedek uvmishpat uv'chesed uv'rachamim
V'erastikh li b'emunah v'yada'at et Adonai.
I betroth you to myself forever; I betroth you to myself in righteousness and in justice, in love and
     in mercy;
I betroth you to myself in faithfulness, and you shall know G-d.

From The Protestant Wedding Sourcebook

In the presence of God and before our family and friends,
I, Sam, take you, Alex, to be my [wife/husband].
All that I am I give to you, and all that I have I share with you.
Whatever the future holds, I will love you and stand by you,
as long as we both shall live.
This is my solemn vow.

Quaker

In the presence of God and these our Friends, I take thee to be my [wife/husband], promising
     with Divine assistance to be unto thee a loving and faithful [husband/wife] so long as we both
     shall live.

SECULAR WEDDING VOWS

What follows is a collection of thoughtful, articulate wedding vows written and shared by the readers of APW.

I, Sam, commit myself to you, Alex, as [wife/husband] to learn and grow with, to explore and adventure with, to respect you in everything as an equal partner, in the foreknowledge of joy and pain, strength and weariness, direction and doubt, for all the risings and settings of the sun.

We tie these knots to symbolize our connection to one another. They represent our trust in each other and our combined strength together.

* * *

Today, surrounded by people who love us, I choose you Alex to be my partner. I am proud to be your [wife/husband] and to join my life with yours. I vow to support you, push you, inspire you, and above all love you, for better or worse, in sickness and health, for richer or poorer, as long as we both shall live.

* * *

OFFICIANT: Do you, Sam and Alex, pledge to create a life of mutual respect, compassion, generosity, and patience toward each other as you grow together in years?

COUPLE: We do.

OFFICIANT: Do you pledge to recognize each other's individuality and celebrate each other's uniqueness as a strength in marriage. While at the same time, will you guard one another's weaknesses with understanding, support, and inspiration?

COUPLE: We do.

OFFICIANT: And do you pledge to share the love you have for each other with all living beings? To be a couple that lets their marriage radiate into others, making their lives more beautiful because of it?

COUPLE: We do.

OFFICIANT: Sam/Alex, if you will face each other and repeat after me:
Alex, I give you my life. With all that I am and all that I have, I honor you.
Sam, I give you my life. With all that I am and all that I have, I honor you.

* * *

continues —

I, Sam, take you Alex to be the wife/husband of my days, the companion of my house, the friend of my life. We shall bear together whatever trouble and sorrow life may lay upon us, and we shall share together whatever good and joyful things life may bring us. With these words, and all the words of my heart, I marry you and bind my life to yours.

* * *

You have taught me that two people joined together
with respect, trust, and open communication
can be far stronger and happier than each could ever be alone.
You are the strength I didn't know I needed,
and the joy that I didn't know I lacked.
Today, I choose to spend the rest of my life with you.
I promise to love you for who you are,
and for who you are yet to become.
I promise to be patient,
and to remember that all things between us are rooted in love.
I promise to nurture your dreams and to help you reach them.
I promise to share my whole heart with you,
and to remember to show you how deeply I care for you,
no matter the challenges that may come our way.
I promise to love you loyally and fiercely—as long as I shall live.
Do you take me to be your lawfully wedded [husband/wife]?

* * *

I, Alex, do pledge you, Sam, my love, for as long as I live. What I possess in this world, I give to you. I will keep you and hold you, comfort and tend you, protect you and shelter you, for all the days of my life.

Gettin' It Done

11

❧ APW BASICS ❧

1. Most people getting married can't afford a wedding planner. However, just because you don't have a wedding planner doesn't mean your wedding doesn't need to be organized and coordinated.

2. Sometime in the vicinity of not-the-last-minute, spend the time to create documents like a wedding timeline, a floor plan, a pack list, and maybe even a seating chart.

3. Although you don't need a rehearsal dinner, you probably do need a wedding rehearsal. Desperately whispering, "What do we do next?" in the middle of the ceremony is less than ideal.

4. You can't manage all the logistics of your wedding day while also trying to have the emotional experience of getting married.

This means you need someone else to be in charge on the day-of.

5. Although you might decide you want to pay someone to run your wedding (a planner or a day-of coordinator), you can absolutely ask a friend or family member to help you out as your wedding stage manager.

◆

T HE FIRST TIME I WAS A BRIDES-maid, the bride spent much of the day rotating between screaming and crying. Needless to say, she didn't enjoy her wedding very much, but no matter what the media would have you believe, she wasn't crazy. She just tried to manage all the logistics the day of her wedding by herself. She was stressed, didn't have enough help, and was trying to have an emotional experience while she coordinated a complex event, which is nearly impossible. As bridesmaids on deck, we stepped in and tried to manage as much of the wedding reception as we could, but with no preparation it was still sort of a hot mess.

My goal these days is to make sure no bride ever cries from stress while waiting to walk down the aisle, and that no bridesmaid ever tries to organize the wedding reception without so much as a timeline from the couple getting married. The one and only solution to these problems? A whole lot of planning.

BEING LAID-BACK REQUIRES ADVANCE PLANNING

The reality is, the modern American wedding takes a lot of logistical organization. And frankly, the more laid-back you want your wedding to be, the more work you probably need to do in advance. If you're not paying a banquet hall and a fancy wedding planner to plan everything for you, someone is going to have to make sure everything from decor to food service is taken care of. And if you don't delegate that role, you and your partner are going to be those people, and you're going to be stressed.

There are a few key parts to making your wedding run smoothly and with minimal tears. First, you'll need to do some serious organization in advance—from timelines to cleanup. Next, you'll want to make sure

that you have all your plans recorded in a cohesive way. In this chapter, we'll review the documents you'll want to prepare. The Appendix provides detailed examples of these documents, so you don't have to reinvent the wheel.

ONCE IT'S PLANNED, PASS IT OFF

Finally, after your wedding is all planned, you'll need someone to help out on the day-of, so you can be freed up to do the emotional work of getting married. While wedding *planning* is all about logistics, wedding *having* is all about emotions.

If your wedding is small, passing it off might mean you hand over your cell phone and the restaurant reservation for your celebratory lunch to your BFF before you head up the courthouse steps. But for many weddings you'll either want to pay a professional day-of coordinator (DOC) or ask a friend to help out in the unofficial (but vital) role of stage manager. (For more, see page 58.)

HOW LONG IS A WEDDING?

Wedding guests will give part of their day to your wedding, but at a certain point they'll get tired and leave (and you might be *exhausted* and want to leave). It's silly if you've paid for your venue for twice as long as needed. If you know that a handful of your friends will want to party till dawn, book a bar for an after party or just meet up at one. However, for the main wedding, plan on time frames that look more like this. (And remember, you'll need to book your venue for longer than these time frames, because you need to allow time for setup and breakdown.)

> **Saturday-Evening Wedding:** Generally five to six hours, seven hours max
> **Cocktail-Style Wedding:** Four to five hours
> **Daytime or Weekday-Evening Wedding:** Four to five hours

As always, know your crowd. If you and many of your close friends will be able to party for eight hours, go ahead and plan for it. If a lot of kids are involved, keep bedtimes in mind.

A WEDDING TIMELINE IS A GIFT TO YOUR GUESTS

For most parts of wedding planning, I'll encourage you to think about your own needs, then consider other people's needs, and come to a compromise. When it comes to wedding timelines, however, I'm going to encourage you to consider other people first.

A good timeline takes care of people, gets them fed on time, and minimizes how long they have to stand around thinking, "Are they done taking photos already or what?" It builds guest activities into times when you'll be otherwise busy (they drink while you pose!) and ensures that people

won't arrive at the reception at 6:00 p.m., hungry for dinner, but not have food put in front of them until a ravenous 9:00 p.m.

When you start putting together a timeline, you'll want to make a general one (like the examples that follow), and then plug it into a timeline spreadsheet that allows you to detail who is doing what, and when (see pages 212–213).

I've included some specific timelines to help you construct your own, but in addition, here is a general list of activities that you should be considering.

• **Hair, makeup, and other prep**— Whether you're doing your own hair and makeup or having a stylist primp you and all of your best people, every planner in the world warns that this activity almost always runs behind, so allow more time than you think you need.

- **Leaving for the venue**—You know how it always takes you longer than you think to get out of the house for a party? On your wedding day, allow for even more time than that. Also make sure you allocate more than enough time to get to your venue (or to any site where you're going to take photos, and then to your venue), even with traffic.

- **A pre-wedding photo session**—Not so long ago, it was traditional for the couple to not see each other before they walked down the aisle. These days, whether or not a couple has an officially photographed first look, many couples take photographs together before the ceremony, which has two benefits. First, this lets you see each other in a more intimate way before you're in front of a throng of loved ones. Second, it lets you get a good chunk of your posed portraits out of the way so you can spend more time enjoying this party you're throwing.

- **Setup**—If your wedding is being set up by professional vendors, they'll know exactly how long they need and be able to work within any venue limitations. If friends and family are taking care of prep, make sure you formulate a more detailed plan to guarantee everything is ready in time. (And be realistic. On average, it takes thirty minutes to set up tables and chairs, so if you have a bunch of additional decor, either allow for a lot of people to help or extra time.)

- **When the venue needs to be guest ready**—Guests will inevitably start arriving up to thirty minutes early (and will continue arriving a little late). Given that, make sure that you're comfortable with how your venue will look about half an hour before the official start time.

- **Ceremony start time**—Plan on a start time fifteen minutes after the time stated on the invite. No matter what, people will be late. (And shocked if you start right on time.)

- **The ceremony**—Try to run through your ceremony a few times in advance (even if this just means reading it out loud), to get a grip on what a realistic run time will look like. Also realize that if a non-pro is officiating, the ceremony time will be more unpredictable. Allow some for that.

- **Moving from the ceremony to the reception**—If your reception is taking place in one location and your ceremony is taking place in another, make sure that you allow ample time for everyone (guests, wedding party, and the two of you) to move from one location to the other. The two-location wedding takes a bit more planning, as you need to make sure that your reception site is set up and ready to go when guests arrive. It's best to start with something like cocktails, which will fill time as guests trickle in. Also, keep in mind that cocktail hour is often used for group and family photos, so find space for that in your schedule. Whatever you do, make sure you provide clear directions to the next location, and allow plenty of wiggle room for things like traffic, and guests getting lost.

- **Post-wedding photos**—Some couples may decide to do all of their posed photos after the ceremony (and if you do this, you should make sure your guests are being fed and watered while you're busy), but even couples that take their photos early should consider allowing for a few photos after they're hitched. Once the threshold of OH MY GOD WE'RE MARRIED NOW has been crossed over, take a few photos in that new emotional state. If you are getting married in the afternoon, photographers love to do portraits around sunset ("the golden hour") for good reason— the light is beautiful.

- **Cocktail hour**—A cocktail hour doesn't have to be an hour, and it doesn't have to include cocktails. Its real purpose is buffer time. This allows you time to change the space over if the ceremony and reception are in the same room. It also allows you to take whatever photos you didn't take before the wedding. And it can run long or be cut short if you're running off schedule.

- **Moving people from cocktails to food (or food to the dance floor, or . . .)**— The process of herding tipsy wedding guests is a bit like herding drunk kittens. Make sure you build in a bit of buffer time every time you're going to try to get people from one activity to the next.

- **Meal**—Although the meal itself will probably only take about forty-five minutes, you need to plan enough time to get everyone served. If you're having a buffet, keep in mind that they always take a little longer than planned. (A general estimate is roughly twenty minutes per fifty people.) If you're serving a plated or family-style meal, it tends to take about twenty minutes to serve fifty to sixty guests, and it will take thirty to forty minutes to serve more than a hundred guests.

- **Toasts**—Toasts can take place during the meal, if you're having one, or just after. Figure out who wants to make a toast beforehand, so things don't devolve into an endless open-mike night. Make sure someone is in charge of passing the microphone along to the next speaker. You probably want to remind people to keep speeches down to a few minutes in length and suitable for all audiences, but you know your crowd.

- **First dance**—No one is going to dance till the couple has taken the floor. So do your first dance first. If you want to do parent-child dances, schedule them directly after, and then open the floor.

- **Additional rituals**—You may be planning on having additional traditions in

·•· PRO TIP ·•·

Remember that your vendors, namely, your photographer and your coordinator if you have one, need to eat. That means you need to provide twenty minutes before the toasts or after the toasts for them to do so, before you move on to the next event that needs to be photographed, like the first dance.

your reception, from a bridal bouquet toss, to the hora, to a dollar dance. Regardless of what traditions you're including, it's wise to include them on the timeline. Although their placement doesn't have to be exact, it's helpful to know that you're planning on the hora taking place about an hour into the dancing.

- **Cake cutting**—One old-fashioned wedding tradition that endures is the cake cutting as the signal that the formal wedding events are done, and guests are free to leave. As strange as it may sound, people still follow this rule. This means scheduling your cake cutting isn't as simple as "dessert comes right after dinner!" but is instead something of a strategic choice. If you perform the ritual cake slicing early, you

may lose some guests directly after. And if you cut the cake very late, you'll have grumpy older guests waiting (and waiting) for the cue that they can leave. If you want a raging dance party, you may want to schedule your cake cutting before the real party starts to allow for an unbroken flow of music. If you want to hang on to guests a little longer, take a break in the dancing to cut the cake.

- **Event end time**—While you might *want* to party all night long, chances are good that you need to be out of your venue by a particular time. Allow for fifteen to thirty minutes of guests packing up and leaving, an hour of breakdown, and end the party accordingly. Doing a formal send-off is a great way to signal that the wedding is, in fact, over (and to get out of there before cleanup starts). If you don't want to leave in such a structured way, turn off the music and turn up the lights, and people will get the idea.

SAMPLE TIMELINES

Evening Wedding

10:00 a.m.—Hair and makeup/Getting ready begins

12:00–2:00 p.m.—Most vendors arrive for setup

2:00 p.m.—Wedding party and family photos start

3:30 p.m.—Doors open/Guests begin to arrive/Pre-ceremony music starts

4:00 p.m.—Invite time

4:15 p.m.—Ceremony starts

4:35 p.m.—Ceremony ends

4:40 p.m.—Cocktail hour starts

5:45 p.m.—Move guests into dinner

6:00 p.m.—Buffet opens/Dinner served

6:35 p.m.—All guests have food

7:00 p.m.—Toasts

7:15 p.m.—First dance

7:25 p.m.—General dancing music starts

8:30 p.m.—Cake Cutting

9:45 p.m.—Last call

9:55 p.m.—Music off

10:00 p.m.—Guests depart

10:00 p.m.—Breakdown commences

11:00 p.m.—Everyone out

Morning Wedding

7:00 a.m.—Hair and makeup starts

8:00 a.m.—Vendors arrive/Setup starts

9:15 a.m.—Couple's portraits

9:30 a.m.—Family pictures

9:45 a.m.—Guests begin to arrive

10:15 a.m.—Invite time

10:30 a.m.—Ceremony starts

11:00 a.m.—Ceremony concludes

11:00 a.m.—Cocktail hour starts

12:00 a.m.—Lunch is served

12:15 p.m.—Toasts

12:45 p.m.—Cake cutting

12:50 p.m.—First dance

1:00 p.m.—Dance party

2:40 p.m.—Last dance

2:45 p.m.—Send-off

3:00 p.m.—Guests depart

3:00 p.m.—Breakdown commences

4:00 p.m.—Everyone out

Cocktail Wedding

1:00 p.m.—Vendors arrive for setup

2:30 p.m.—Guests begin to arrive

3:00 p.m.—Invite time

3:15 p.m.—Ceremony starts

3:30 p.m.—Ceremony ends

3:35 p.m.—First round of food comes out/Bar opens

3:35 p.m.—Music starts inside

5:00 p.m.—Heavier rounds of food come out

5:15 p.m.—Toasts

5:30 p.m.—First dance

6:00 p.m.—Pre-sunset portraits

6:30 p.m.—Cake cutting

7:00 p.m.—Couple and guests depart

7:00 p.m.—Breakdown commences

8:00 p.m.—Everyone out

THE GAP BETWEEN RELIGIOUS CEREMONIES AND RECEPTIONS

What happens when the time you're offered at the church is 11:00 a.m., and the earliest your venue can start the reception is 3:00 p.m.? Couples and guests have dealt with this since time immemorial, so if you're stuck with a similar schedule, everyone will survive. When finalizing your schedule, keep in mind that a longer gap is actually better than a shorter gap. With an hour in between, guests can't grab lunch, but with three hours they can get both lunch and a nap.

Here are some strategies from Meg Hotchkiss of La Vie En Rose Events for smoothing the transition:

> Have a receiving line outside the church. They're traditional, but mostly they take up time, while letting you greet all of your guests.
> Give your guests some suggestions of what to do between the ceremony and reception. This could be as simple as guiding them toward good lunch spots, or pointing them toward interesting local sites they can check out.
> If you're booking a hotel block, make sure you book it in a place that's easy to get to in between the events. The real truth of the matter is that most of your guests are going to want to take their shoes off and rest.

·✦· PRO TIP ·✦·

Jesse Tombs, a senior event producer at Alison Events, says that you should give a copy of your floor plan to all of your vendors, so they'll know exactly where everything should be. (Including things like flower arrangements, which can easily be marked on this layout.)

MAKING A FLOOR PLAN

A floor plan is a way to map out your space, make sure you have enough room, and know where everything is going to go. Remember that you don't just need to account for the tables people will be sitting at but also things like the dance floor, buffet tables, gift table, drink tables, and a bar.

If you have a caterer, a wedding planner, or are getting married in a full-service venue or at a restaurant, one of your vendors or venue staff may take care of creating a floor plan for you. If you don't, you may be on your own.

To get started, you'll need the floor plan from your venue, or the dimensions, along with useful information like where electrical outlets are located. After that, it's mostly a bit of math.

How Much Space Do You Need?

When it comes to laying out your space, it's all about the numbers. Have you seated your guests far enough from each other that they can pull out their chairs?

- To calculate whether your venue is big enough for your guest list, keep this in mind: in a room, you need ten square feet of space per person for dining only, and fifteen square feet of space per person for dining and a dance floor with a band.
- Dance floors themselves should have roughly three square feet per guest. (That said, keep in mind that not everyone will be dancing, and you can work with whatever you've got.)
- Each person needs about two feet of table space for the most comfortable seating (for example, an eight-foot long rectangular table ideally should have four people per side).
- Chairs are between eighteen and twenty inches wide and deep. So from the edge of the table you need to leave eighteen inches per chair, and at least sixteen inches between the backs of chairs. (Allow thirty inches if your meal will be served by waiters instead of buffet style.)
- On buffets, allow two feet per food container. You will need one table and one staff person to prep and maintain the buffet per hundred guests.

- If you are serving family style, account for the amount of space the platters will occupy on the table. Also, consider keeping centerpieces very small, or cutting them entirely.

WHEN TO HAVE A SEATING CHART

It's easy to dismiss seating charts as something you'd only do if you were having a big formal wedding, but I'm unabashedly pro seating charts for most weddings where a meal is being served. Unlike most parties you throw, at your wedding, everyone won't know most everyone else. And when all those people from all those various parts of your life finally get together, it's good to give them the feeling that you've got their backs (and that they won't end up sitting alone with a group of your ninety-year-old great-aunts).

There are several ways to do seating charts, and some instances when you just don't need them.

When to assign tables and seats: When you have complicated family dynamics. When you want to do some matchmaking. When you have really long tables. When you have a plated meal where people have picked their entrées in advance. When you have a plated meal and people with food allergies or dietary restrictions. When you have a really formal wedding.

·•· PRO TIP ·•·

Alyssa Griffith of Rose Gold Events suggests that your name cards should be color coded (or otherwise coded with symbols) if you need to let your waitstaff know who is receiving what meal, or who has dietary restrictions.

·•· PRO TIP ·•·

Meg Hotchkiss of La Vie En Rose Events suggests that you color code your Post-it flags by type (family, partner A friends, partner B friends, mutual friends, or whatever categories make sense to you).

When to assign tables, but not seats: When you have reasonably sized round tables. When your family is going to rearrange all of the name cards anyway. When you want to save yourself a little work.

When to skip the seating chart: When you're having a mix-and-mingle reception like a cocktail or a cake-and-punch shindig. (Note: Even if you're not assigning tables, it's wise to reserve a few tables and chairs for older people or people with health or mobility issues. Make sure you tell those folks in advance that they have seats reserved.)

ESCORT CARDS, NAME CARDS, AND HOW SEATING ASSIGNMENTS WORK

You need a simple way to get all of your guests to the appropriate tables and seats without causing half an hour of confused milling about. The simplest way to do this is with escort cards, along with name cards if you're assigning seats.

To create an escort card board (or clothesline, or wall), create cards for all of your guests, listing their names and their table numbers. Attach these to a board in alphabetical order, and let people take their own cards to their seats. If there are no table assignments, these escort cards can serve as guests' place cards. If there are assigned seats, they'll find place cards at their tables, designating their spots.

CREATING YOUR SEATING CHART WITH MINIMAL TEARS

Sadly, your seating chart will not descend from the heavens with the perfect solution for how to keep Aunt Mindy away from Uncle Buddy. Nope, you're going to have to create the damn thing. Wait till you have most of your RSVPs to start working on your seating chart, but not so long that suddenly it's the night before the wedding.

There are a lot of digital tools online that can help you create a seating chart, and you should use them, if that's the way you do your best work. Personally, I'm a fan of hands-on seating chart creation: blow up a copy of your floor plan, put your guests' names on Post-it Page Markers, and move the flags around till things more or less make sense. You can also label index cards by table, and use exactly the same Post-it method without a giant floor plan.

When you've finalized your arrangement, you'll want to copy it onto a paper seating-chart plan, as well as create an alphabetical and by-table list. You can use this list to create name cards with things like Avery cards that you can print at home, but regardless, you'll want to file these lists away in your day-of binder. (See pages 181–182.)

PLANNING A WEDDING WEEKEND

As friends and family are increasingly spread out geographically, it's become more common to turn weddings into a weekend-long reunion of sorts. Sometimes this means just offering a welcome reception and possibly a morning-after brunch, but it can also entail a three-day campsite retreat.

If you're planning a wedding weekend without a dedicated wedding planner running everything for you, go easy. Planning a wedding is hard enough. Planning a wedding and six other meals and ten other events might kill you.

With that in mind, a few pointers:

> **Delegate.** Just like you can't manage all the logistics of your wedding day while actually getting married, you (really) can't manage a whole weekend on your own. If you're able to hire a team of professionals to pull this off, more power to you. But if you can't, put different volunteers in charge of different projects. Uncle Glenn can manage Saturday breakfast. Crafty Kate can set up Saturday night's wedding decor. Auntie Beth can host Sunday brunch.

> **If you want to maximize attendance at events, try to have everyone stay in one location.** This could mean renting out a campsite for the weekend, or booking a big block of rooms at a particular hotel. (And remember, as with everything else weddings, you can't control your guests' choices. They might end up staying elsewhere.)

> **Do not plan every moment of every day for your guests.** People will want to do things on their own, or just chill out and catch up with old friends. Build in some breathing room.

> **Make activities optional.** Sure, your guests might want to go on that boating trip.

— *continues* —

But they might also want to prowl around on their own and find the best local taco place.

> **Don't feel that you have to provide every meal** (unless you have everyone at a remote summer camp with no access to outside food). Also remember that some of your meals can be low key, like a DIY sandwich bar.

> **Don't plan activities too late, or too booze focused, the night before the wedding.** You know exactly why that is.

> **Communicate, communicate, communicate.** Wedding websites were made for wedding weekends. Let everyone know as much of the schedule as possible in advance, with details. Let your guests know if they're on their own for breakfast, or if what you're providing is a simple continental buffet. Tell them if that boat trip is not open to toddlers and exactly what it costs. Provide advice on local favorite spots that they might want to hit up on their own. Give people enough early information that they can make plans.

> **Limit exclusive events.** If you want to have a dinner out with just your bridesmaids, consider doing that the night before everyone arrives. Once everyone is in one place, your job is to be a good host, and that includes not having parties that the majority of people are not invited to.

> **Don't overplan your *own* weekend.** Remember, you're getting married, and that's an exhausting and wonderful occasion on its own. Plan on giving yourself the downtime you need, so you can go into your wedding well rested and present.

·✦· PRO TIP ·✦·

If you're not providing transportation but you're worried that some of your guests might not be super sober at the end of the night, consider providing taxi or public transportation information, both on your wedding website (if you've got one), and on an obviously placed sign at the venue. You can also set someone on sobriety duty, making sure everyone with plans to drive is, in fact, sober enough to drive.

SHUTTLES, BUSES, AND VINTAGE CARS

Full disclosure: Wedding transportation can be kind of complicated. But I'll let you in on a trade secret. You don't have to provide wedding transportation for, well, anyone. It's not traditional; it's not part of good etiquette; it's not even part of the unwritten wedding contract. Adults are very good at getting themselves to and from places (and even navigating that issue when they're not sober). They will manage just fine for your wedding.

However, it's possible you *want* to provide some transportation. Maybe you want your bridal party to travel together during the wedding day. Maybe your wedding is in a remote area, and you want to provide transportation for the whole group. Or maybe, for some reason, your venue just requires it. In that case, let's walk through the logistics of transportation organization.

- When coming up with a transportation plan, check local events, conference, and sports dates around your venue. If you happen to be getting married three blocks away from the Grammy Awards, transportation might suddenly become much more important because there will be zero parking available.
- Determine how many seats you will need. Early RSVPs are helpful, as are online questions asking if guests will use the transportation. However, all things being equal, you're probably going to have to guess. This means you want to find a company that has a good cancellation or change policy, and then try to slightly overestimate how many people will use transport.
- Many transportation services require a minimum number of hours. That may mean that setting up transportation in just one direction is not particularly cost efficient. In some cases, however, you can arrange for "one-way transport" that consists of exactly one trip.
- Always ask your transportation company for the names and phone numbers of the drivers in the days before the wedding. Provide these to your wedding stage manager (pages 58–59),

·✦· PRO TIP ·✦·

Alyssa Griffith from Rose Gold Events says that it's important to be incredibly clear and detailed when providing your written transportation timeline to a service, both for getting a quote and for arranging for actual transport. She says, "This document should have the date, the time they arrive, the time guests load, the time they leave the first location, time they arrive at the second location (leave room for traffic, error, etc.), and so on. This is one of the most logistically detailed pieces of a wedding, especially if there are multiple locations, multiple vehicles, etc. Be precise and detailed to ensure that the company has all the information so that it runs smoothly and successfully." (If this seems overwhelming, just remember that you can always skip transportation entirely.)

your day-of coordinator, or a helpful volunteer.

- When informing guests of the timing for shuttle pickups, give them a time at least ten minutes before the actual time the shuttle will leave. Tell them (nicely) that they can't be late or they'll (literally) miss the bus.

- Assign a friend or family member to be the point of contact at every pickup spot (and provide their cell-phone information to your drivers). Ideally, give them lists of everyone being picked up at their stops, so you can make sure nobody is left behind.
- As with all important vendors, work with good reviews and recommendations. As someone who nearly missed her prom due to a shoddy limo service, I can attest that you don't want your guests to miss the ceremony because of terrible transportation.

THE WEDDING REHEARSAL

You don't want people to realize five minutes before showtime that they don't know what to do, or where to stand. So unless you are eloping or having a five-minute ceremony, you should probably have a wedding rehearsal. It doesn't need to be at your venue and it doesn't need to involve your officiant, if those things are not possible. But it should happen, and it should involve as many of the major players in your ceremony as you can round up.

Here is the wedding planner cheat sheet for making a wedding rehearsal happen as painlessly and quickly as possible.

- **Have someone (who isn't you) be in charge.** You might not have a planner or a day-of coordinator, but that

> **·➤· PRO TIP ·➤·**
>
> Event planner Meg Hotchkiss of La Vie En Rose points out that the rehearsal is your last chance to take stock of what you need for the ceremony. She says, "Make sure there is a place for everyone and everything. Do you need a table for a sand ceremony? Make sure there's a table." Although you might not be in your wedding venue, running through the ceremony should still give you a chance to make sure that your checklist of ceremony items contains everything it should.

doesn't mean you want to be shouting orders at your wedding rehearsal. Pass over all your plans to someone else, and let that person call the shots.

- **Start with announcements.** You have all your key players in one place, ready to take instruction. Use this time well. Let people know the timeline for the next day, where and when they need to be prior to the ceremony, and if they need to report for family or group photos. This is also a good time to remind them to do commonsense things like turn off their cell phones prior to the service, take gum out of their mouths, not wear sunglasses, and not slouch or put hands in their pockets (if you at all care).

- **Run the rehearsal in reverse.** Put the key players in their ceremony spots, run through the ceremony, then do the recessional, and finally do the processional. That way everyone knows what spot to head to.
- **Give people cues for the processional (and recessional).** If you're not going to have someone to tell people when to start walking down the aisle on the day-of, take this opportunity to give people a cue as to when they should begin. This could be a musical cue, but it

---

•→· PRO TIP ·→•

Allie Shane of Pop The Champagne says, "I like to make it clear that once the rehearsal is over, the celebration starts for the couple—no more logistics, no more planning, no more questions. Give people the opportunity to ask as many questions as they want during the rehearsal, confirm getting-ready times, outfit choices, or hand out printed timelines…whatever you need to do to ensure you aren't getting phone calls the morning of, asking about socks and boutonnières."

---

might just be "when the couple ahead of you gets a third of the way down the aisle." Do the same for the recessional. You don't want the wedding party rushing for the back of the venue en masse the second after you kiss.

- **Hit the high points.** Your goal here isn't to re-create the whole ceremony (or blow your possibly secret vows). Instead, you're running through the blocking. Who stands where, and when, and what do they do?

THE REHEARSAL DINNER

Do you have to have a rehearsal dinner? Or if you do throw a party the day before the wedding, does it have to be a rehearsal dinner, exactly? The answers to both questions are *probably* no, but the real answer is that this is going to depend on your crowd, as well as regional and social expectations. In short, only you and your partner (and possibly your family) know the answers to these questions.

The rehearsal dinner has long been the property of the parents. And though a lot has changed about weddings, this hasn't totally. Which is often a good thing, because let's be for real, you can't throw two weddings in one weekend. As such, the party the day before the wedding gives you a great space to compromise. Your in-laws wanted a formal wedding, and you're getting married on the beach? Hand them the rehearsal dinner. Your mom really wanted to serve lobster, but you're going vegetarian? Throw her a claw the day before. The upside to this is that parents who get what they want at the rehearsal dinner generally have to pay for it.

But that isn't to say your rehearsal dinner has to be everything your mother-in-law wants. It doesn't even have to be a dinner at all. The reason to have a party the day before you get married is to get an additional—and much more laid-back—chance to see all those people you love who came together to see you get hitched. When you think of it that way, it opens up a world of options. Here are a few:

- **Welcome picnic:** Have your family throw something on the grill, or hire a caterer who will come BBQ for you affordably, and invite everyone who wants to come.
- **Pizza and beer:** Host this at a pizza place, or at someone's house. With pizza and beer, you basically can't go wrong.
- **Rehearsal lunch:** It doesn't have to be at night.
- **Family-style dinner:** This can be at someone's house or a restaurant, and it can be as formal or informal as you'd like.
- **Small dinner followed by open invite at a bar:** Have just the wedding party and family come to a small dinner, and then tell everyone what bar you'll be at, and when. (Just be careful to moderate

> **·←· PRO TIP ·→·**
>
> Meg Hotchkiss from La Vie En Rose Events says, "I recommend that like items are packed together—a box for ceremony stuff, a box for cocktail hour, a box for reception. Label all these boxes clearly with the location and contents. That way, when they're loaded in, they can be easily distributed to the right area."

how much you and the key players drink the night before, because, hangovers.)

GETTING ALL THE STUFF THERE, AND BACK AGAIN

Forget fluffy tulle and beautiful letterpress invitations. In reality, putting on a wedding often feels like it's mostly about managing the stuff. Even if you're attempting to have the most laid-back wedding in the world, my God does there still seem to be a lot of stuff! Booze, compostable dinner plates, decorations, your parents' heirloom silver cup—all of it has to be accounted for, carted to the venue, set up, packed up, and then carted away. If you can make a plan for organizing and transporting all this stuff well before the panicked week before the wedding ("How many people do we know with pickup trucks again?"), you're in good shape.

Here are some steps for managing all those objects, and generally organizing setup and breakdown.

- **Create a pack list.** This spreadsheet (see pages 206–207) should include a comprehensive list of all wedding-related items, who's getting each thing there (and back), where it will be used during the wedding, and whether it will be discarded or brought home. For extra organizational prowess, you might want to number the boxes that you're sending to the venue and mark which box each item is in.
- **Make specific people in charge of specific important items.** If you're bringing any important family heirlooms, don't trust them to a cardboard box. Put a particular family member in charge of each treasured item.
- **Find out if you can drop items off at your venue early.** Some venues will store a few clearly labeled boxes in advance of your wedding, which can help logistics on the day-of.
- **Consider renting a cargo van (or organize well in advance who is hauling what items).** There are distinct advantages to transporting everything in one vehicle, namely, if one of your four friends with a pickup truck bails on you

the day before, you're not in big trouble. But what's most important is simply that you come up with a cohesive plan for getting everything to your venue and back well in advance of your wedding.

- **Figure out where you can park to unload items into your venue.** Speak to your venue to figure out what the best way of unpacking things is going to be.
- **Check your venue's load-in requirements.** When are you allowed to load in? Do you have to use a freight elevator? Does everything have to get walked up a tiny set of stairs? Check to make sure you know all the rules the venue has about load-in, and run your general setup plan by them.
- **Plan your setup.** Come up with a realistic timeline for how long it will take to set things up, and how many people you will need. Don't be afraid to ask a lot of questions of vendors. For example, the rental company may be able to give you a time estimate for setup, even if they're not doing the heavy lifting. Unless you have the venue for a long period in advance of the wedding, try to avoid decor projects that involve complex or time-consuming installation. Once you've come up with realistic estimates for time and labor, create a detailed list in your timeline document (see pages 212–213 for an example) of who is doing what, and when.

- **Know when your venue needs to be guest ready.** Guests generally start showing up about thirty minutes in advance of the ceremony, so aim for key areas being more or less set up by then.
- **Figure out if you need the reception set up during or after the ceremony.** In an ideal world, your wedding will take place in one convenient location, with two separate spots for the ceremony and the reception. In reality, this might not be the case. If your venue needs to be flipped (the ceremony space needs to be transformed into a reception space during cocktail hour), plan for that. If your reception is separate from your ceremony site and loved ones are setting it up, make sure you've planned time for them to make it to the actual wedding.
- **Assign people who are going to be sober enough to break down the wedding (and drive).** Breaking down a wedding is much easier than setting it up. Half of the items will have been used up or eaten or discarded, but you'll still need a relatively sober person to lead the charge. Everything remaining (plus whatever gifts were brought to the wedding itself) should be neatly packed up and returned to the location listed on the pack list (you may want all items to be deposited at a friend's or family member's home, where you can

collect them a day or two later). Anyone involved with striking the wedding should agree to help in advance, because carting away boxes is not a fun drunken surprise.
- **Confirm when you need to be out of the venue, and what state the venue needs to be returned to.** You don't want to be stuck with an extra charge because you took two hours to clear out of the venue instead of the allotted single hour, or because the venue wasn't broom swept. Make sure you know the requirements, and that your sober pack-out leader understands them as well.

DAY-OF EMERGENCY KIT

Planners show up to a wedding with an emergency kit, which is one of the reasons they're paid the big bucks. Ever wonder what's in those magic bags? Here is a crazy comprehensive list, straight from the source. You should not go out and buy every item here. Instead, pick items that seem like they would be helpful to you, and pack them away in one easy-to-find place. Also, make sure you know where the nearest drugstore is, and have a friend who's ready to run out to pick things up as needed.

All that said, if you're DIYing your wedding setup, look seriously at the first section of the list. You might not need eyelash glue, but chances are good you'll need gaffer's tape, because life just works like that.

DIY, DECOR, AND THE KITCHEN SINK

> Glue: superglue, hot-glue gun
> Tape: Scotch, painter's, gaffer's
> X-Acto knife
> Command hooks
> A few pairs of scissors
> Pens and markers
> Fishing line (for hanging things)
> Zip ties, wire
> Stick lighters
> Box of matches
> Mini tool kit
> Envelopes
> Petty cash

PERSONAL

> Safety pins
> Eyelash glue
> Earring backs
> Hairspray
> Bobby pins
> Comb
> Brush
> Hair elastics
> Black shoelaces
> Extra black socks
> An undershirt
> Styptic pencil
> Deodorant
> Shout wipes
> Sewing kit
> Static guard

> Lint brushes
> Chalk (for stains on white shirts or wedding dresses)
> Mints
> Chewing gum
> Dental floss
> Mouthwash
> Tissue packets

MEDICAL

> Tylenol
> Benadryl
> Band-Aids
> Tampons/pads
> Contact solution
> Eyedrops
> Tweezers

THE WEDDING PLANNING BINDER

After you've organized the hell out of your wedding, your job is to compile all of your planning documents into one binder and pass them to someone else to manage things on the day-of.

Below is a comprehensive list of what you might want to have in your day-of binder. Some of these documents won't apply to you, and you might think of additional documents that you want. The goal is simply to pull as much of your planning together as you can, so that someone else can answer all of those pesky logistics questions, and you can say your vows and party.

- Vendor list: All vendors and their contact information. Remember that the person you have been communicating with might not be the day-of contact, so make sure you have the cell-phone number of the latter.
- Important people list: Wedding party, family, and so forth, and their contact info
- Timeline: Detailed enough for anyone to follow
- A few copies of a general timeline: To be handed to vendors (or pushy family members) as needed

- Transportation documents
- Pack-in/Pack-out lists
- Floor plan
- Decor plan, as needed
- Photography must-have shot list (if you have one)
- Ceremony script, including processional order
- Extra copies of the vows
- Marriage license
- Seating chart, list of guests and table assignments, meal-list choices
- Menu and beverage list
- List of which people are giving toasts
- DJ song list, if special songs have been requested (or discouraged)
- All your vendor contacts

Conclusion: From Here to the Stars

A ND THEN, ONE DAY, JUST LIKE that, you're married. It's time to give away all those hot-pink tissue paper puffs, figure out how to clean a vintage dress/feather cape/custom suit, and send some heartfelt thank-you notes. And then, it's really over.

As much as planning can be the world's biggest pain in the ass, afterward, there are a few moments when life can feel a bit empty. What did you do, back before your weekends were full of shopping for hard-to-find birch chuppah poles and frantically assembling seating charts? What project should you embark on together next?

Well, the real project ahead of you is simply this: your marriage. It's the reason

you went through all this planning in the first place, the reason you made the vows, the reason you planned that whole party.

Popular culture will tell you that your wedding is the best day of your life (and quietly insinuate that it's all downhill from there), but they're fumbling their lines. In theory, maybe (maybe!) your wedding was the best day of your life . . . *so far*. (But then again, maybe it wasn't.)

On our wedding day, my husband gave me a note. In it, he said that he hoped this would not be the best day of our lives. His dream was that it would simply be the first day of our lives as a married couple, with many more good days to come. Of course, he was right.

As messy and imperfect, joyful and transcendent as our wedding day was, it was simply one important day in a long string of important days together. Since then, we've had (just like the vows promise) better and worse. The wedding day is just one beautiful patch in that patchwork quilt.

So sweep up the glitter. Box up the dress. Take a moment to mourn the passing of your wedding (and to celebrate the passing of the wedding *planning*). And then move forward together. Because there is so much more to be done.

HOW TO THROW A WEDDING IN A NON-TRADITIONAL SPACE

If you're throwing a wedding in a non-traditional space, here is the list of tasks that you should consider. (For more details see pages 35–36.)

- ☐ Research permits
- ☐ Research parking
- ☐ Research noise ordinances
- ☐ Check facilities (bathrooms, kitchens, etc.)
- ☐ Check with the neighbors
- ☐ Get event insurance

POTENTIAL RENTAL ITEMS CHECKLIST

If you have a full-service caterer or an all-inclusive venue, you may never have to worry about renting tables, chairs, or glassware. But for those of you who have rentals on your to-do list, here is a starter list of items to consider. Your rental company will provide you with a much more detailed breakdown, but consider this a place to start. (For more on rentals see pages 36–41.)

TABLES AND CHAIRS

- ☐ Dining tables (long, round, square)
- ☐ Cocktail tables
- ☐ Buffet tables
- ☐ Cake table
- ☐ Bar tables
- ☐ Head table
- ☐ Sweetheart table (a table just for two)
- ☐ Chairs (for ceremony and for reception; may be possible to use the same chairs)
- ☐ Chair covers

LINENS

If you want to upgrade something, nicer linens can be a good investment. Cotton looks much nicer than poly, and colored napkins can be a great way to add decorative punch to a table without any extra work.

- ☐ Reception tablecloths
- ☐ Buffet, cake, and bar tablecloths
- ☐ Napkins

DINNERWARE

This is generally not a particularly worthwhile place to upgrade, as food covers the plates in short order. Include some extras for breakage.

- ☐ Dinner plates
- ☐ Salad and bread plates

- ☐ Cake plates (if you're serving dessert, remember you'll need an additional set of plates)
- ☐ Place settings

GLASSES

Estimate 2 to 3 glasses per type per guest, up to 5 to 6 glasses per person. Remember your guests will walk away from their drinks, and running out of glasses puts a damper on a party.

- ☐ Water glasses
- ☐ Wine glasses
- ☐ Champagne flutes
- ☐ Bar glasses

SERVEWARE

- ☐ Serving dishes
- ☐ Serving implements
- ☐ Warmers

VARIOUS

- ☐ Tent
- ☐ Generators
- ☐ Lighting
- ☐ Amplification (for self-DJing, or just a mike and amp for the ceremony and toasts)
- ☐ Port-a-potties

DIY CATERING CHECKLIST

Note: This checklist is designed for parties where the food is professionally prepared but not served by a full-service caterer. (For more on self-catering see pages 85–87.)

- ☐ Figure out what rentals you need: Tables, chairs, plates, serving dishes, linens, flatware, warmers.
- ☐ Figure out if there is any serveware you want to purchase: Compostables? Disposables?
- ☐ Organize and figure out staffing: How many people will you need to help out, and in what roles? Can you fill all of these slots with reliable family and friends? Do you need to hire additional help, whether local teenagers or professionals from a catering staffing company?
- ☐ Scheduling: Create a clear schedule for setup and cleanup.
- ☐ Will you be purchasing alcohol? If so, see pages 79–81 for a buying guide.
- ☐ Figure out what event insurance you might need, particularly if you are serving alcohol. (See page 36 for more on event insurance.)
- ☐ Figure out a food safety plan. Ideally, ask someone to complete online food safety training and to monitor on the day-of.
- ☐ Figure out trash disposal. Will you need to provide your own trash cans and garbage bags? Will you need to cart garbage away at the end of the night?

POTENTIAL FLORAL ITEM LIST

When you're trying to figure out what flowers you want, it can be helpful to look at a list of common options. Do you need all of these? Absolutely not. In fact, if you're DIYing your flowers, I suggest picking as small a selection of flowers as possible. This list exists because it can be helpful to remember that, yes, you do want flowers for your cake, or the bathroom, or your puppy, and make note of that.

PERSONAL FLOWERS

- ☐ Bouquet(s) for bride(s), any attendants, and possibly toss bouquet(s)
- ☐ Flower crown(s)/Flowers for hair
- ☐ Flower kid items (petals, crown, mini bouquet, pomander)
- ☐ Boutonnière(s) for partners and attendants
- ☐ Ring bearer items—boutonnière, collar for dog, flower crown for your cat (I'm joking! Am I?), and so on
- ☐ Florals for parents/grandparents/guests of honor—bouquets, corsages, boutonnières
- ☐ Florals for officiant/ushers/ceremony participants—boutonnières/corsages

CEREMONY

- ☐ Entryway/Welcome/Guest book table
- ☐ Altar/Chuppah/Arch/Backdrop
- ☐ Pew/Chair/Aisle
- ☐ Petals for tossing

RECEPTION

- ☐ Cocktail tables
- ☐ Bar
- ☐ Escort card table or display
- ☐ Guest book and favor tables
- ☐ Guest table centerpieces
- ☐ Special chair decor
- ☐ Buffet table/Food station
- ☐ Cake table/Cake decor
- ☐ Restrooms
- ☐ Getaway car

DIY FLOWERS SHOPPING LIST

BOUQUETS, CORSAGES, AND BOUTONNIÈRES

- ☐ Floral pins
- ☐ Rubber earring backs (to put on the ends of exposed pins)
- ☐ Floral tape (the stretchy, self-adhering kind)
- ☐ Floral wire (to reinforce stems and for boutonnières)
- ☐ Ribbon
- ☐ Heavy scissors or shears
- ☐ Wire cutter
- ☐ Hot-glue gun
- ☐ Rose thorn stripper
- ☐ Buckets, trash cans, or something else with water in it for storage and transportation

CENTERPIECES AND DECOR

- ☐ Waterproof floral tape (the clear kind for vases)
- ☐ Floral foam
- ☐ Flower food
- ☐ Heavy scissors or shears
- ☐ Rose thorn stripper
- ☐ Buckets, trash cans, or something else with water in it for storage and transportation

DIY BAR ALCOHOL-BUYING CALCULATIONS

of drinking age guests _____ x # of hours of open bar time _____
= _____ *total # of drinks needed (one per person per hour)*

BEER AND WINE ONLY

_____ # of drinks needed x .25 = _____ # of beers needed
(Purchase bottles, or calculate the number of kegs needed, based on 165 servings per keg.)
_____ *# of bottles needed*
_____ *# of kegs needed*

_____ # of drinks needed x .75 = _____ # of glasses of wine needed
(Divide this number by 4 to get the total number of bottles of wine needed.)
_____ *# of bottles of wine needed*
(For a winter or evening wedding, estimate 40% red, 30% white, 30% sparkling. For a summer or daytime wedding, estimate equal numbers of red, white, and sparkling.)

FULL BAR

_____ # of drinks needed x .5 = _____ # of glasses of wine needed
(Divide this number by 4 to get the total number of bottles of wine needed.)
_____ *# of bottles of wine needed*
(For a winter or evening wedding, estimate 40% red, 30% white, 30% sparkling. For a summer or daytime wedding, estimate equal numbers of red, white, and sparkling.)

_____ # of drinks needed x .2 = _____ # of beers needed
(Purchase bottles, or calculate the number of kegs needed based on 165 servings per keg.)
_____ *# of bottles needed*
_____ *# of kegs needed*

_____ # of drinks needed x .3 =_____ # of cocktails needed
(Divide this number by 18 to get the total number of bottles of alcohol needed.)
_____ *# of 750ml bottles of alcohol needed*
(Get a mix of dark and light liquors.)

DIY BAR ALCOHOL-BUYING SHOPPING LIST

WINE

☐ Red

☐ White

☐ Sparkling

BEER

☐ Light

☐ Dark

☐ Microbrew

HARD ALCOHOL (At least one from each category)

☐ Dark (bourbon, Irish whiskey, etc.)

☐ Light (gin, vodka, etc.)

☐ Extras (tequila, brandy, rum, specialty, etc.)

MIXERS

☐ Soda (club soda, cola, etc.)

☐ Juice (orange, cranberry, etc.)

☐ Fruit

☐ Garnish

DIY BAR SETUP LIST

If you're DIYing your bar setup, chances are good that you're going to remember to buy booze. You'll probably even remember to buy mixers. But it's easy to show up at your venue and realize that not only did you forget ice, you forgot towels, and your bar helpers are looking murderous.

   When you head to the store for alcohol, take this list with you. As always, use your judgment. This list is designed to be comprehensive, and depending on your setup, you might not need every item.

- ☐ Ice
- ☐ Large ice buckets or coolers for keeping beer and wine chilled (unless your venue has refrigeration at the bar site)
- ☐ Ice storage vessel for top of bar—a deep tray, bucket, or other receptacle
- ☐ Garnish storage for top of bar—bowls, Tupperware, and the like
- ☐ Towels (at least two per bartender, plus more for keeping surfaces clean—they typically come in packs of twenty-four)
- ☐ Speed-pour tops—one per booze type (optional, but makes it easier and faster for your bartenders to pour)
- ☐ Cutting board
- ☐ Bar knife
- ☐ Straws, skewers, and napkins, as needed
- ☐ Any garnish supplies your drinks require (for example, if you're serving margaritas, provide a rim plate and lots of salt)

One per bartender of the following:

- ☐ Wine key
- ☐ Ice scoop
- ☐ Bottle opener
- ☐ Cocktail shaker
- ☐ Sturdy pint glass for shaking
- ☐ Strainer
- ☐ Stir spoon
- ☐ Jigger
- ☐ Citrus squeezer

FINAL SITE VISIT/VENUE WALK-THROUGH CHECKLIST

- [ ] What are the space/room measurements?
- [ ] Get a copy of a typical (or planned) layout of the space.
- [ ] Discuss how the day will flow. Actually picture guests coming in. Where will they go? Do they need directional signs?
- [ ] What decor can you hang? How can you hang it? What items do you need to purchase to execute your design plans?
- [ ] How high are the ceilings? Will you need to bring a ladder or step stool?
- [ ] Review any rental items the venue is supplying.
- [ ] Confirm what items (if any) the venue will set up and tear down.
- [ ] Where and how do the vendors load in? Confirm timing.
- [ ] Where and how do vendors and family and friends load out? Confirm timing.
- [ ] Confirm all cleaning and pack-out protocol.
- [ ] Where are the power outlets (specifically in relation to planned band or DJ and lighting setup plans)?
- [ ] Will you need extension cords?
- [ ] Test any built-in or included sound systems with your proposed music plan (iPod, laptop, etc.). Ensure you have all necessary cords.
- [ ] Confirm any restrictions (candles, decor, space, etc.).
- [ ] Confirm contingency plans in case of weather changes.
- [ ] Ensure you have the name and day-of contact information for the venue coordinator.
- [ ] Confirm any final payments due to venue.

LAST-MINUTE THINGS YOU MIGHT HAVE FORGOTTEN (TWO WEEKS OUT)

- ☐ Delegate anything that hasn't been delegated yet. If you're planning on doing it yourself on the day-of, find someone else to do it. (By now, you probably know why.)
- ☐ Figure out what payments are still owed and get them squared away. Some payments won't be due until the day-of, so make sure to delegate those payments to someone else (including tips).
- ☐ Get any clothing you'll need cleaned or pressed.
- ☐ Finalize your day-of (and weekend) timeline and give it to any VIPs who will need to know where everyone is (this includes vendors, important family members, and anyone who will be helping out).
- ☐ Pull together emergency day-of contact numbers for vendors and important family members.
- ☐ If you haven't given your photographer a list of important family members or required family portraits, send a list via e-mail.
- ☐ Get your marriage license.
- ☐ Arrange transportation back from the reception for you and your partner, as needed.
- ☐ Assign people to help with venue setup and breakdown.
- ☐ Figure out who will be taking home anything left over.
- ☐ Start packing for your honeymoon, if applicable.

LAST-MINUTE THINGS YOU MIGHT HAVE FORGOTTEN (NIGHT BEFORE)

(Rip this list out, and stick it to your front door, or the door to your hotel room.)

☐ Rings
☐ Vows
☐ Marriage license
☐ Dress(es)
☐ Suit(s)
☐ Driver's license
☐ Wallet
☐ Cash
☐ Bra, socks, and underwear
☐ Other jewelry and accessories
☐ Comfortable shoes to change into later
☐ Tips for vendors (hand off to someone you trust to give them out)
☐ Wedding playlist (if you made your own)
☐ Umbrella (just in case)
☐ Snacks and water

If you're staying the night:

☐ Toothbrush and toothpaste
☐ Birth control/condoms
☐ Something to sleep in
☐ Outfit for tomorrow (don't forget underwear and a regular bra)
☐ Honeymoon luggage (if applicable)
☐ Passport (if applicable)

LIST OF DOCUMENTS TO HAVE IN YOUR DAY-OF BINDER

- ☐ Vendor list (with contact numbers)
- ☐ Important people list (with contact numbers)
- ☐ Timeline(s) (include extra copies)
- ☐ Transportation information
- ☐ Pack-in/Pack-out lists
- ☐ Floor plan
- ☐ Seating chart (visual and spreadsheet, including important food choices or mobility requirements)
- ☐ Decor list and setup plan
- ☐ Photography shot list
- ☐ Ceremony script
- ☐ Copies of vows
- ☐ Marriage license
- ☐ Menu and beverage list
- ☐ List of who is giving toasts
- ☐ DJ song list
- ☐ Copies of vendor contracts
- ☐ Copies of permits and insurance forms

SAMPLE SPREADSHEETS

These sample spreadsheets will help you set up your own organizational tools for your wedding. If, however, you don't want to reinvent the wheel, you can find downloadable versions of all of these documents (plus exclusive bonus documents) at apracticalwedding .com/planner.

GUEST LIST AND SEATING CHART – SAMPLE SPREADSHEET

TITLE	FIRST NAME	LAST NAME	E-MAIL ADDRESS	HOUSEHOLD	ADDRESS	POST CODE	PHONE NUMBER	
Ms.	Beyoncé	Knowles	beyonce@ sashafierce.com	The Knowles-Carter Household				
Mr.	Shawn "Jay-Z"	Carter	jayz@thebomb .com	The Knowles-Carter Household				
Ms.	Blue Ivy	Carter		The Knowles-Carter Household				
Ms.	Joanne	Woodward	jo@newmansown .com	Paul Newman & Joanne Woodward				
Mr.	Paul	Newman	paul@ newmansown.com	Paul Newman & Joanne Woodward				
Dr.	Jane	Goodall	monkeydoc@gmail .com	Dr. Jane Goodall & Guest				
	Guest			Dr. Jane Goodall & Guest				

SAVE THE DATE SENT	INVITATION NUMBER*	# ATTENDING WELCOME EVENT	# ATTENDING WEDDING	TABLE#	MEAL CHOICE	DIETARY RESTRICTIONS	GIFT	THANK-YOU SENT

BUDGET – SAMPLE SPREADSHEET
TOTAL PROJECTED BUDGET: $XX,XXX

	BUDGETED TOTAL COST (INCLUDING TAX)	ACTUAL TOTAL COST (INCLUDING TAX)	AMOUNT OVER/ UNDER BUDGET	DEPOSIT AMOUNT PAID	
Venue, Food, and Beverage					
Venue (ceremony)					
Venue (reception)					
Catering/Food (including food, service, flatware, stemware, china, etc.)					
Bartending/Beverage (including service, alcohol, glassware, etc.)					
Cake/Dessert (don't forget cutting fees!)					
Ceremony Specifics					
Marriage license					
Officiant					
Ceremony music					
Photography/ Videography					
Photographer					
Videographer					
Decor					
Flowers (personal and decor flowers)					
Other decor, etc. (candles, guest book, ring pillow, etc.)					
Lighting					
Rentals (tables, chairs, linens, dance floor, etc.)					

PAID BY?	BALANCE DUE AMOUNT	FINAL PAYMENT DUE DATE	WHO IS PAYING?	NOTES

— continues —

Total Projected Budget (continued)

	BUDGETED TOTAL COST (INCLUDING TAX)	ACTUAL TOTAL COST (INCLUDING TAX)	AMOUNT OVER/ UNDER BUDGET	DEPOSIT AMOUNT PAID	
Stationery/Paper Goods					
Save-the-Dates					
Invitations (including RSVP cards)					
Other (menu, program, escort cards, etc.)					
Postage					
Attire					
Outfits and accessories for two people!					
Don't forget hair and makeup costs.					
Entertainment					
DJ/Band/etc.					
Planner/Coordinator					
Miscellaneous/Other					
Transportation, photo booth, gifts, favors, extra fees, etc.					
Tips					
Emergency Fund					
Always try to have at least 5–10% set aside, just in case.					
TOTALS					

PAID BY?	BALANCE DUE AMOUNT	FINAL PAYMENT DUE DATE	WHO IS PAYING?	NOTES

VENUE SEARCH – SAMPLE SPREADSHEET

VENUE NAME	LOCATION	CAPACITY	AVAILABILITY	TYPE	LAYOUT	RATES	

	WEBSITE	RESTRICTIONS	PARKING / TRANSPORTATION	FACILITY EXTRAS	CATERER

PACK LIST – SAMPLE SPREADSHEET

GENERAL ITEMS	QUANTITY	BOX NUMBER	LOCATION FOR WEDDING	GOES HOME WITH...
Pre-Ceremony Partner 1				
Dress/Suit	1	freestanding	Hotel Room	On Sam
Headpiece	1	freestanding	Hotel Room	On Sam
Jewelry	1 necklace, 2 earrings, 3 bangles	freestanding	Hotel Room	On Sam
Shoes	1 pair	freestanding	Hotel Room	On Sam
Ring	1	freestanding	Hotel Room	On Sam
Pre-Ceremony Partner 2				
Dress/Suit	1	freestanding	Hotel Room	On Chris
Shoes	1 pair	freestanding	Hotel Room	On Chris
Tie, cuff links, etc.	1	freestanding	Hotel Room	On Chris
Ring	1	freestanding	Hotel Room	On Chris
Ceremony				
Flowers	4 bouquets, 3 boutonnières, 15 centerpieces	freestanding	Parents' House	Given to guests
Decorations	40 tissue paper poufs	4	Parents' House	Parents
Wedding signs	4 boards	freestanding	Parents' House	Parents
Chuppah poles	4	freestanding	Parents' House	Parents
Chuppah cover	1	1	Parents' House	Parents
Chuppah base	4	freestanding	Parents' House	Parents
Programs	2 boxes	2	Parents' House	Parents

continues —

GENERAL ITEMS	QUANTITY	BOX NUMBER	LOCATION FOR WEDDING	GOES HOME WITH...
Reception				
Cake cutter	1	1	Parents' House	Parents
Garter	1	1	Parents' House	Parents
Escort cards	1 box	2	Parents' House	Parents
Escort card board	2	freestanding	Parents' House	Parents
Guest book, pens	1 box	2	Parents' House	Parents
Glue, scissors	1 box	2	Parents' House	Parents
Tape/Scissors/Knife	1 set	2	Parents' House	Parents
Kids' table kits	5	2	Parents' House	Parents
Etc.				
Sewing kit	1	1	Parents' House	Parents
Deodorant, etc.	1	1	Parents' House	Parents
Hairpins, supplies	1	1	Parents' House	Parents
Emergency kit	1	1	Parents' House	Parents
Step stool	1	freestanding	Parents' House	Parents

IMPORTANT PEOPLE – SAMPLE SPREADSHEET

NAME	RELATIONSHIP	CELL PHONE NUMBER	FLIGHT INFORMATION	

	ARRIVAL TIME	DEPARTURE TIME	WHERE THEY'RE STAYING	NOTES

VENDOR LIST – SAMPLE SPREADSHEET

ROLE	BUSINESS NAME	CONTACT NAME	DAY-OF CONTACT NUMBER	COMMITMENT(S)	
Photographer				8 hours with 2 photographers and photo booth	
Wedding stage manager/DOC				10 hours, 1 assistant, plus setup, breakdown, and vendor management	
Bar company				3 kegs, 24 bottles of wine (12 red, 12 white), plus 1 bartender	
Bakery				3-tier cake, 75 cupcakes	
Officiant				30 minute ceremony, will bring copies of readings	

	ARRIVAL TIME	ADDITIONAL INFO	GETS MEAL?	FINAL PAYMENT STATUS	TIP?
	2:00 PM		Yes		Will send by mail
	Noon		Yes		$200, with DOC
	Noon		No		No
	2:00 PM		No		$20 for driver, with DOC
	3:00 PM		No		Donation at later date

WORKING TIMELINE – SAMPLE SPREADSHEET

WHEN	WHAT	WHERE	WHO
Pre-Ceremony			
11:00 AM	hair & makeup	Getting Ready Room	couple, partner B's sister
12:30 PM	stuff gets picked up from house	couple's house	wedding stage manager/DOC
1:00 PM	venue opens	venue	wedding stage manager/DOC
1:15 PM	catering staff arrives	venue, inside	caterer
2:00 PM	sound system arrives/is set up	venue, inside	DJ or sound system rental
2:30 PM	couple & photographer arrive for pre-ceremony pictures	venue, outside	photographer, couple
2:30 PM	florist arrives to set up flowers	venue, inside	florist
2:30 PM	alcohol arrives	venue, inside	partner A's brother
3:00 PM	family arrives for pictures	venue, outside	photographer's assistant
3:00 PM	cake delivered	venue, inside	bakery
3:00 PM	couple & family pictures	venue, outside	photographer, couple, family
3:30 PM	couple finishes pictures, goes inside	Getting Ready Room	couple
Ceremony			
3:45 PM	guests start to arrive	venue, outside	ushers
4:00 PM	official start time on invites	venue, outside	
4:15 PM	processional	venue, outside	wedding stage manager/DOC cues
4:35 PM	recessional	venue, outside	rabbi
Cocktail Hour			
4:40 PM	alone time for couple	Getting Ready Room	couple
4:40 PM	cocktail hour starts	venue, inside	wedding stage manager/DOC, caterer
4:55 PM	couple post-ceremony pictures	venue, outside	photographer, couple
5:15 PM	couple joins cocktail party	venue, inside	couple
Reception			
6:00 PM	guests seated for dinner	venue, inside	caterer cues
6:10 PM	first guests to buffet	venue, inside	wedding stage manager/DOC cues
6:30 PM	last guests through buffet	venue, inside	wedding stage manager/DOC cues
6:30 PM	toasts—four total	venue, inside	wedding stage manager/DOC cues

— *continues* —

WHEN	WHAT	WHERE	WHO
Reception (*continued*)			
7:10 PM	first dance	venue, inside	wedding stage manager/DOC cues
7:10 PM	dance party!	venue, inside	DJ
8:00 PM	cake cutting	venue, inside	wedding stage manager/DOC cues
8:10 PM	Hora/ritual dances	venue, inside	DJ
8:10 PM	dance party!	venue, inside	DJ
9:40 PM	last call	venue, inside	wedding stage manager/DOC cues
9:50 PM	send off	venue, outside	wedding stage manager/DOC cues
10:00 PM	guests out	venue, inside	wedding stage manager/DOC cues
Post-Reception			
10:00 PM	caterer/wedding stage manager/DOC/family start breakdown	venue, inside	wedding stage manager/DOC
10:20 PM	families leave with stuff they're taking	venue	families
12:00 AM	breakdown done, everyone out	venue	wedding stage manager/DOC

DECOR SETUP INSTRUCTIONS – SAMPLE SPREADSHEET

NAME/TITLE	ITEMS NEEDED	BOX #(S)	DESCRIPTION	WHO?
Guest tables	mason jars, candles, table numbers, menu cards	1, 3, 5	Pre-decorated mason jars to be filled with flowers on the morning of, placed in groups of three on each table. 5 votive candles per table. 1 table number per table (see floor plan). 1 menu card per place setting.	Ashley
Escort card display	large frame with wires hung, clothespins, escort cards, easel	2	The frame and easel will be freestanding, not in boxes. They should be set up as close to the double doors entering the hall as possible. Clothespins and escort cards are in box two and should be hung in alphabetical order inside the frame from the wires.	Joe

FIND MORE RESOURCES ON APRACTICALWEDDING.COM

If you just finished the book, the first thing you should do is go take a nap. Seriously. But, as you're starting to put your wedding together, chances are there are going to be more questions you need answered and problems you want solved. And for that, there's APracticalWedding.com. APW is the living, breathing companion to this planner, so if there's something you can't find in here, you can definitely find it over there. Here's just a little of what you can find on APW:

Planning Tools and Logistical Advice: I've packed as much logistical advice into this planner as I could manage, without creating a multi-volume wedding encyclopedia. (Because who wants that?) For more detailed tips on how to do things like create a timeline, or write a ceremony, or plan a rehearsal dinner, head to APW's planning and logistics sections.

Tutorials: Once you've figured out the *what* of decor, the next step is the *how*. Sure, Pinterest is chock full of pretty ideas, but on APW, we break everything down into easy, affordable projects that you can actually, you know, do yourself (without a team of professional stylists).

Downloadable Spreadsheets: No need to reinvent the wheel. You can download all of the spreadsheets referenced in this book at apracticalwedding.com/planner.

Real Weddings: Whereas most wedding websites do weddings like magazine spreads (big on pictures short on information), our real weddings section is filled with useful tips from couples, plus real weddings planned on actual budgets.

Vendors: If after reading Chapter 4, you've decided you want to hire professional vendors for your wedding, the next step is . . . actually hiring them. APW has one of the best vendor communities online. The business owners in our vendor directory must sign a sanity pledge saying that they won't treat you like a walking dollar sign (and that they are LGBTQ friendly). So if you are in search of a photographer or day-of coordinator, or anyone else for that matter, head to apracticalwedding.com/vendors and you may find what you're looking for.

Marriage Content: This book can help you plan your wedding, but only you can plan your marriage. We keep the conversation going on APW, with frank discussions about careers, relationships, sex, money, and anything else you want to talk about.

I'll see you there!

Acknowledgments

A BOOK LIKE THIS ISN'T POSSIBLE WITHOUT A TEAM. MY TEAM INCLUDED researchers, fact checkers, suggestion makers, editors, sanity maintainers . . . and an OBGYN. Because if books are like babies, you might as well do both at once, amiright?

My profound gratitude for making this book possible goes to one kick-ass group of ladies. To Alyssa Griffith of Rose Gold Events, for her tireless research assisting and encouragement, not to mention her constant patience with me as I picked her brain. I committed to doing this book the moment she agreed to help me, in a warehouse hung with a fluffy cloud installation, and am so glad we made it a reality. To Maddie Eisenhart, APW's deputy editor and my right-hand lady, for her constant flow of ideas, determination, and shared ambition, not to mention her nearly flawless running of the website on days when I was up to my ears in words. To Kate Bolen, for her copyediting and gut checking, and helping midwife this book into the world, just like she did my last one. To Dana Eastland, for stepping up in the ninth hour to project manage, research, fact check, and deal with reams of paperwork.

Beyond that, I have to thank the staff of APW past and present, for giving me the time to take on this enormous project. Not only did they continue maintaining the site I'm proud to call my online home, they grew it like crazy when they could have just kept up the status quo. Thanks goes (again) to Maddie Eisenhart, and Kate Bolen, along with Kerianne Kohler, Najva Sol, Liz Moorhead, Lucy Bennett, and our whole team of interns, writers, and contributors. Further, many thanks go to our readers, who constantly inspire and challenge me. Without the many women who have made up the community of APW over the years, no one would ever have believed that we women wanted something like . . . sane weddings.

I'm consistently and constantly grateful to my agent, Maura Teitelbaum, who believed in these books even when no one else did and has faith in me even when the publishing industry seems like a grim place to be. A huge confetti-filled thank-you to my editor, Renee Sedliar, who made writing this book more fun than it had any right to be (and reminded me that fun wasn't always the point). Also, a cheer for her being the only editor within ten minutes of my house, and one I was lucky enough to land.

They say the people you love the most only gather when you hatch, match, and dispatch, and your wedding is especially meaningful because—of those three moments—it's the only one you'll remember. As I wrote this book about matching, my life was filled with hatching and dispatching. This is for our daughter who screamed her way into the world, and for my father-in-law and grandmother who quietly left, just as the book was entering it.

But from the bottom of my heart, my deepest gratitude goes to my own little family, which holds my place in the world. To David, who gave me the first idea for APW and is my tireless cheerleader, hand holder, and partner in everything. From that magical warm August day in the hills, till now, I'm so grateful for what we've built. To J., whose tiny self is full of boundless love, enthusiasm, and support unlike any I've ever known. And to L., who was with me every moment of every day writing this book, and exploded into our hearts like a firework shortly after I put down the proverbial pen. This book is theirs, as much as it is mine.

A HUGE THANK-YOU TO THE MANY WEDDING PLANNING PROFESSIONALS WHO allowed me and my team to take far too much of their valuable time to interview them for this book—and who passed on tons of information that is often kept a closely guarded secret. They include:

Alexis Adams, manager, Esqueleto Oakland
Michael Antonia, owner, The Flashdance
Elizabeth Clayton, owner and principal, Lowe House Events
Jennifer Colgan, co-owner, The Wedding Party
Liz Coopersmith, Silver Charm Events
Jessica Dixon, owner, The Petal Company
Anita Dolce Vita, editor in chief, Dapper Q
Isabelle Donovan, event coordinator, Duvall Events
Dana Eastland, food writer
Michelle Edgemont, owner and creative director, Michelle Edgemont Designs
Maddie Eisenhart, digital director and style editor, A Practical Wedding
Nikol Elaine, owner, Nikol Eliane Makeup Artistry
Alison Faulkner, The Alison Show
Justin Fone, executive producer, Justin Fone Productions

Nicole Fredrichs, owner and lead wedding specialist, Playa Bliss Weddings

Yazmin Gizeh, Sea of Dreams Weddings

Alyssa Griffith, owner and lead planner, Rose Gold Events

Jesi Haack, owner and designer, Jesi Haack Design

Corie Hardee, owner, Little Borrowed Dress

Tori Hendrix, Sitting In A Tree Events

Julia Henning, vice president of sales and marketing, Wedgewood Wedding & Banquet Centers

Meg Hotchkiss, founder and lead planner, La Vie En Rose Events

Tabitha Johnson, owner, Winston & Main

Kristy List, pastry chef

Suzanne Marinez, owner, Lang Antique and Estate Jewelry

Natalie Marvin, owner, Belle-Flower

Amberly Odom, owner, Wrennwood Design

Carly Rae, owner and lead stylist, Carly Rae Weddings

Molly Schemper, head pastry chef and owner, FIG Catering

Oran Scott, owner, Relic Vintage

Allie Shane, lead party animal, Pop the Champagne

Lauren Smith, Hourglass Productions

Jesse Tombs, senior event producer, Alison Events Planning & Design

Katie Wannen, The Plannery

Chrissy Wolfman, catering sales manager, InterContinental Mark Hopkins

Leon Wu, founder and CEO, Sharpe Suiting

Thanks also go to those who have lent their expertise to APracticalWedding.com, as well as to this book. They include:

Genevieve Dreizen, officiant, Cheerleader For Love

Jen Girdish, writer

Yesenia Guinea, San Francisco hairstylist

Alyssa Mooney, APW contributor

Ali Noland, attorney

Elisabeth Snell, APW contributing writer

Hayley Tuller, APW contributor

Taryn Westberg, founder, Glosite.com